CLEAN SLATE

A COOKBOOK AND GUIDE

Reset Your Health,
Detox Your Body,
and Feel Your Best

CLEAN SLATE

A COOKBOOK AND GUIDE

Reset Your Health,
Detox Your Body,
and Feel Your Best

Clarkson Potter/Publishers
New York

Selected photographs and recipes appeared in previous Martha Stewart Living publications.

All rights reserved.
Published in the United States
by Clarkson Potter/Publishers,
an imprint of the Crown Publishing Group,
a division of Random House LLC, a Penguin
Random House Company, New York.
www.crownpublishing.com
www.clarksonpotter.com

CLARKSON POTTER is a trademark
and POTTER with colophon
is a registered trademark of Random House LLC.

Library of Congress Cataloging-in-Publication Data
is available upon request.

ISBN 978-0-307-95459-6
eBook ISBN 978-0-307-95460-2

Printed in China

Book and cover design by Jennifer Wagner
Cover photographs by Johnny Miller

Photograph credits appear on page 319.

10 9 8 7 6 5 4 3 2 1

First Edition

INTRODUCTION 8

PART ONE
reset

_____

GET A CLEAN START 12

GOLDEN RULES FOR EATING CLEAN 14

KNOW YOUR NUTRIENTS 36
super detoxifiers 39
antioxidant powerhouses 41
inflammation fighters 43
digestive aids 45

RESTOCK YOUR PANTRY 46
smart swaps 47
whole grains 48
legumes 53
healthy fats 56
flavor enhancers 59

DETOX YOUR MIND AND BODY 60
3-day action plan 62
21-day action plan 64

PART TWO

recipes

---

replenish

get off to a good start
73

reboot

drink to your health
109

recharge

load up on your vegetables
119

reenergize

choose your snacks wisely
185

restore

make meals with substance
213

relax

have a little something sweet
293

BASICS 314
SOURCES 316
ACKNOWLEDGMENTS 318
PHOTO CREDITS 319
RECIPE INDEX 320
INDEX 326

introduction

Most of us know that the way we eat is central to our well-being. But we may not always know exactly what ingredients to buy or meals to plan for the most satisfying, delicious, and healthful results. This book will show you how easy it can be: Start with fresh produce, whole grains, and lean proteins; prepare them simply; and take the time to share and enjoy them.

This old-fashioned approach to food has a modern name—eating clean. It means making meals from scratch, whether a workday breakfast for one or a weeknight dinner for four. It means making your own snacks instead of relying on anything from a package. And it can also mean enjoying dessert (see Golden Rule 11: Maintain a Healthy Perspective, page 34)! Just as important, eating clean means focusing on every aspect of our meals—turning away from our screens and devices and avoiding other distractions, so we can savor the process of cooking and eating.

Perhaps you're already eating this way, or maybe these ideas are new to you. Either way, there is plenty to discover here. You'll find excellent recipes as well as the very latest advice from reliable professionals, including nutritionist Kathie Madonna Swift, who contributed her knowledge and expertise to this project. I'm still exploring and evolving and looking for new ways to appreciate clean, whole food, and I hope you'll be inspired to do the same.

Martha Stewart

reset

GET A CLEAN START

Whatever inspired you to pick up this book—a resolution to eat better, a desire to wipe the slate clean with a whole-body detox, or a wish to boost your energy level—you have just taken the first step toward achieving that goal. This book is designed for anyone wanting to hit the reset button and gain a more rewarding, and pleasurable, approach to food.

Food plays a central role in our lives. On the most basic level, it feeds our hunger and keeps us alive. But it also functions on social and emotional levels, so to fully address nutrition you need to consider, from all angles, what you eat. Focusing on whole, unprocessed foods helps your body prevent and fight diseases and increases your energy levels. This means eating fresh fruits and vegetables, beans and other legumes, whole grains and whole-grain pasta, nuts and seeds, and modest amounts of lean proteins, including fish, eggs, chicken, and tofu. And yes, even the occasional dessert.

As you evaluate what you eat, you should also consider your relationship to food, in terms of how you plan your meals, how you shop, how you prepare food, and how you actually eat it. In our grab-and-go lifestyle, food can become mere fuel to get us through the day, rather than providing us an opportunity to slow down, switch gears, eliminate distractions, and relish the moment.

HOW TO USE THIS BOOK

"Know Your Nutrients" on page 36 lists foods that are the best sources of antioxidants and anti-inflammatory, detoxifying, and digestive properties. Having a well-stocked pantry is an essential first step, and we've covered the basics—whole grains, legumes, healthy fats, and flavor enhancers—in the "Restock Your Pantry" section starting on page 46. Then, we encourage you to clean the slate with one of the action plans (designed for either three days or twenty-one days) outlined on pages 62 to 69. Or you can just start cooking from the wealth of delicious recipes in the second part of this book. But before you do anything else, read the "Golden Rules for Eating Clean" on the following pages, and remember that the goal is a healthy, whole, wonderful appreciation of food, not deprivation.

ABOUT THE RECIPES

In keeping with widely accepted ideals of "eating clean," none of the recipes in this book contains any butter, refined sugar, all-purpose flour, or red meat. Honey and other natural sweeteners appear, as do whole-wheat flour and pasta, and dairy products; full-fat dairy is the most minimally processed, but you can use reduced-fat varieties if you prefer. Look for the icons listed below on each recipe page; these are indicated by colored dots in the Action Plan menus and on the juice and smoothie recipes in the "Reboot" chapter.

ICONS

- VEGAN
- DAIRY-FREE
- NUT-FREE
- GLUTEN-FREE

choose whole foods over processed

Whole foods—primarily fresh fruits and vegetables, whole grains, and legumes—deliver the vitamins, minerals, phytonutrients (plant compounds such as flavonoids and carotenoids), and fiber you need to feel your best.

ABOUT PROCESSED FOODS

Foods that have been processed have been stripped of some or all of their essential nutrients, making them poor substitutes for whole foods. The preservatives that manufacturers add can make matters worse.

Take, for instance, the high amount of sodium found in many processed foods, which has been linked to high blood pressure and heart disease. All the added sugars can cause obesity, diabetes, and blood-sugar spikes that can trigger inflammation. Plus, processed foods often contain artificial colorings and flavorings, chemical preservatives, and additives that can negatively impact our health (and our environment).

Volumes of studies have connected the standard American diet, and its high proportion of processed foods, to epidemics such as cardiovascular disease, autoimmune disorders, gastrointestinal illnesses, and certain types of cancer. According to Kathie Madonna Swift, M.S., R.D.N., L.D.N., an integrative medical nutritionist and former nutrition director at Canyon Ranch in Lenox, Massachusetts (among other leading institutions), "Multiple mechanisms are at play here, including shifting to a pro-inflammatory state, insulin resistance, hormone disorders, and digestive problems, which affect all the systems of the body."

WEIGH YOUR OPTIONS

Don't be fooled by the clever packaging of so-called health foods. According to Marion Nestle, professor at the Department of Nutrition, Food Studies, and Public Health at New York University, "Research shows that almost anything with a health claim—no trans fat, gluten-free, probiotics, or organic—makes people think the food is healthier and lower in calories. A junk food with a health claim, alas, is still a junk food." While no one is suggesting avoiding packaged goods altogether, Nestle recommends "avoiding anything with more than five ingredients, ingredients that you can't pronounce, or anything artificial."

Ultimately, when it's a choice between buying a frozen dinner (even an organic one) and preparing a meal entirely from fresh ingredients, opt for making it yourself, from scratch.

MAKE SMART CHOICES

Some minimally processed foods are better than others, of course—such as canned fish, beans, and tomatoes; plain yogurt; cheese; tofu; and whole-grain bread and pasta. Frozen fruits and vegetables are also worth buying, especially during the months when fresh ones are in short supply. These all offer comparable nutritional value to unprocessed versions, as well as convenience.

embrace a plant-based diet

People who follow a plant-based diet have significantly lower rates of chronic illnesses, including cancer and heart disease, and it's easy to see why: Based primarily on produce, beans and other legumes, whole grains, and nuts and seeds, with modest amounts of fish and other lean proteins, it's a diet rich in health-boosting nutrients.

THE BENEFITS

Besides being an excellent source of vitamins and minerals, the foods in a plant-based diet contain a wide range of antioxidants and anti-inflammatory compounds. (For more specific healthful properties of many of these foods, see the glossaries that begin on page 39 as well as the "Restock Your Pantry" section on page 46). They are also high in dietary fiber that helps rid the body of harmful toxins and helps keep the digestive tract working smoothly. So it should come as no surprise that eating a plant-based diet (similar to the much-touted Mediterranean diet) is strongly linked to lower cholesterol and a reduced risk of obesity, type 2 diabetes, cardiovascular disease, and certain forms of cancer.

CHANGE FOR GOOD

Plus, filling up your plate with plants means there's less room for animal-based foods—and their saturated fats. Butter, cream, red meat, and skin-on poultry are the most obvious culprits. You don't have to cut them out entirely, but rather eat them in moderate amounts.

Once you incorporate more plants into your diet, you'll also find they actually help curb your cravings for sugary sweets and other less-healthy options.

EXPLORE THE PRODUCE AISLE

Rather than sticking with the tried-and-true, experiment with at least two new vegetables or fruits each month, picking what's in season and grown locally, whenever possible. As an alternative to potatoes, try turnips, parsnips, rutabaga, or celeriac; choose mustard, turnip, or collard greens instead of kale or Swiss chard. You can also explore the produce aisles at Asian, Middle Eastern, or Latin American food markets for a wider variety of options.

The more you eat a plant-based diet, the more you will appreciate the way it makes you feel.

practice mindful eating

It's easy to allow your daily intake of food to become more routine than ritual. Instead, slow down and savor every bite—without any distractions. Because when you take the time to focus on what's in front of you, something wonderful happens: You begin to feel more satisfied with less.

FOCUS ON HOW YOU EAT

Make a point to enjoy your meals while seated at the table. Multitasking during a meal—whether that's watching television, working on the computer, or reading a book—can cause you to pile more food onto your plate. If this idea is novel to you, start by sitting down to a distraction-free meal a couple times each week. Soon enough, you'll look forward to the respite that these meals offer from the busyness of life.

Equally as important is how you fill your plate. Imagine produce taking up half, whole grains one quarter, and protein—plant- or animal-based—the remaining quarter. Never feel obligated to clean your plate; it's best to eat smaller, more frequent meals to keep your metabolism on an even keel.

Mark Hyman, M.D., founder and medical director of the UltraWellness Center in Lenox, Massachusetts, suggests eating from a smaller plate, such as one for salads, rather than a standard dinner plate. The portions will be the same size, but the plate will look much fuller.

TAKE YOUR TIME

Don't rush. Allow yourself at least twenty minutes to finish a meal, chewing slowly and thoroughly and making a conscious effort to put your fork down between bites. (Doing so aids digestion.) Tune in to textures, aromas, and flavors, and take pleasure in (re)discovering favorite foods. And learn to appreciate the feeling of being sated without being overly full. This form of portion control, practiced by the inhabitants of the Japanese island of Okinawa (who have one of the highest percentages of centenarians on the planet), is called "hara hachi bu," which roughly translates to "80 percent full."

Before you eat anything, sit down, take five deep breaths, and focus your attention on how your body feels.

engage
in an active
lifestyle

With so much attention being paid to how (and what) you eat, it makes sense to focus on how much you move, too. This is less about committing to a rigorous workout routine and more about taking part in the types of activities that boost your energy, improve your mood, and leave you feeling better than you did before.

GET MOVING

Any type of exercise that gets your heart rate up and creates a sheen of sweat—including yogic sun salutations, brisk walking, and riding a bike—helps your body rid itself of toxins. "Exercise increases blood flow and works your muscles," says Dr. Mark Hyman, "and both of these actions stimulate lymph flow." It is this process, the primary function of the lymphatic system, that helps rid the body of toxins and other harmful substances. (This is why movement is an integral part of the 21-Day Action Plan on page 64.) Exercise has a host of other benefits, too, including promoting better sleep and managing stress, both of which contribute to your overall health.

The energy you expend doing everyday activities like gardening, walking, mowing the lawn, playing tag with the kids, and shoveling snow also adds up. Take the stairs instead of the elevator (try two at a time to really raise your heart rate), and walk or ride your bike to the store instead of driving or using public transportation.

PENCIL IT IN

It's important to establish a routine you can live with. Start by sizing up your schedule and pinpointing pockets of time you can devote to exercising. You should also assess your current fitness level and set goals, whether it's to increase your heart rate or shed a few pounds. Then make a plan. Aim for thirty minutes at least four times a week, even if it means squeezing in three ten-minute stints (in the morning, during lunch, and at the end of a workday)—it counts just the same. Consider steps that will help you stick to your program, like asking a friend to walk with you or joining a running club or a yoga group.

Variety is also helpful in ensuring long-term success, so try to include different activities—such as dancing, Pilates, swimming, or rock climbing. Your body benefits from cross-training, and your mind benefits from the changeup in the routine.

GET THE GREEN LIGHT
Consult with your doctor before embarking on any fitness program or making changes to your activity level.

GO OUTSIDE
If you typically head to the gym, opt for a change of scenery: Studies show that people get more enjoyment and therefore stay motivated longer when exercising outdoors. So head to the local park or beach, seek out nearby hiking trails, or go cross-country skiing.

make sure to get enough fiber

Fiber is absolutely essential to good health: It aids in digestion, regulates blood sugar, promotes a healthy heart, and helps to control weight. "Fiber also feeds the good bacteria in the digestive tract," adds nutritionist Swift, "which helps the immune system protect against invading pathogens (unfriendly bacteria and viruses) and escorts toxins out of the body."

HOW MUCH IS ENOUGH?

Aim for at least forty grams of fiber each day (this is twice the amount in the average American diet). It's actually easy to meet this quota if you eat primarily fruits and vegetables, whole grains (and whole-wheat products), dried beans and legumes, and nuts and seeds. It also means having an orange or grapefruit instead of a glass of juice; topping yogurt with oat-filled granola; adding chickpeas or black beans to salads; and snacking on whole foods such as apples, celery, almonds, and carrots.

SOLUBLE VS. INSOLUBLE

There are two types of dietary fiber—soluble and insoluble. Each plays an important role in keeping your body's systems on track. Both types can make you feel full quickly and for longer. Eat a varied plant-based diet, including all the foods listed at right, to be sure to get both kinds of fiber.

Soluble fiber dissolves in water and binds to and helps eliminate cholesterol, thereby boosting heart health. It also normalizes blood glucose and insulin levels, which can help protect against inflammation and diabetes. Best sources include apples, pears, citrus fruit, and berries; oats, oat bran, and barley; and legumes, carrots, and brussels sprouts.

Insoluble fiber (also known as "roughage") facilitates digestion by increasing the bulk in the stool, which in turn speeds up the elimination of waste and toxins. This type of fiber is found in many fruits and vegetables, but leafy greens like kale, collards, and mustard greens, cabbage, and the skins of apples and pears have the most. Other sources include whole-wheat flour (including that found in bread and pasta), wheat bran, and nuts and seeds.

READ THE LABEL
Whole-wheat and whole-grain products such as bread, cereal, and crackers can be good sources of fiber, as long as you choose them carefully. If there are less than two grams of dietary fiber in each serving, look for something with more. And pay attention to the addition of sugar and other sweeteners, especially high-fructose corn syrup, which can offset the benefits of the fiber.

boost energy with lean protein

Protein provides us with the necessary fuel to power us through the day, promotes brain functioning, and keeps us sated. It's also necessary for building muscles, bones, and cartilage, and every cell in our body needs protein for maintenance and repair. Most Americans (and even vegans) have no problem getting enough protein, but the source of the protein also matters.

TARGET AMOUNT

The Institute of Medicine (IOM), the health arm of the National Academy of Sciences, recommends that protein make up between 10 percent and 35 percent of our daily caloric intake. This translates to about 46 grams per day for an average adult woman, 56 grams for men. To find out your average individual need, multiply your body weight times 0.36. For example, a 110-pound woman should aim for 40 grams of protein per day. As a point of reference, four ounces of cooked salmon has about 26 grams of protein, one cup of cooked lentils about 18 grams, one cup of cooked quinoa about 8 grams, one ounce of pumpkin seeds about 7 grams, and one large egg about 6 grams.

BEST SOURCES

Ideally, you should try to get most of your protein from plant sources; beans and legumes, quinoa, and nuts and seeds are all especially good. Fish is also rich in protein and contains beneficial omega-3s.

Other high-quality animal proteins such as poultry, eggs, and dairy (including yogurt and cheese) can be part of a clean food diet, too: The key is to eat them in smaller quantities and to make smart choices when shopping (see "Know What You Are Buying," page 32).

COMPLETE VS. INCOMPLETE

Animal proteins are considered "complete" proteins in that they contain all nine essential amino acids, the building blocks of protein that must be derived from the food we eat. (Our bodies can produce the other eleven amino acids.)

Soy and quinoa are also complete proteins, but all other plant sources are "incomplete," or missing one or more of these essential amino acids. So long as you eat a variety of these foods every day, you'll be sure to get enough protein in your diet.

A NOTE ABOUT RED MEAT
Although red meat doesn't appear in the pages of this book, or on most clean food lists, that doesn't mean it must be excluded entirely. Just be sure to buy organic, "100 percent grass-fed" or "grass-fed and finished" meats, which contain more omega-3s, vitamin E, and other antioxidants than meat from animals fed corn or grain. Consuming smaller portions (4 ounces, or the size of a deck of cards) and fewer servings per week are also advised.

pay attention to how you feel

Food allergies are rare, affecting only 3 to 4 percent of adults in the United States. Yet food intolerances are on the rise, with many Americans experiencing sensitivities to one or more types of food. Though far less severe than allergies, sensitivities can negatively impact your digestive health as well as your quality of life.

ABOUT SENSITIVITIES

An allergy is an immune-system response that triggers symptoms that tend to come on immediately—from nausea and hives to shortness of breath and anaphylaxis (shock). A food intolerance, on the other hand, triggers a response from the gastrointestinal system that can result in gas, bloating, diarrhea or constipation, nausea, or abdominal pain up to two or three days after consumption.

But since being gassy and bloated after drinking milk or eating pasta does not necessarily mean you have a food intolerance, it's important to avoid self-diagnosis. And restricting your diet unnecessarily can deprive your body of essential nutrients.

Check with your doctor to rule out allergies or other underlying conditions before embarking on an elimination program.

HOW DO YOU KNOW?

According to the American College of Gastroenterology, the primary intolerance culprits are foods containing lactose, gluten, and fructose, but MSG (monosodium glutamate) and other additives, including artificial colors and flavors and artificial sweeteners, are also potential triggers.

If you suspect that any of these are at the root of your symptoms, eliminate them from your diet for seven to ten days, being careful to scrutinize food labels (for instance, modified food starch, malt flavoring, and caramel contain gluten; honey, agave, and fruit juice contain fructose). Take note of whether your symptoms abate, then "re-challenge" your GI system with the suspected culprit. If symptoms return, you're most likely intolerant.

The good news is that even if you're predisposed to intolerance for a food, you can likely eat a certain amount of it without experiencing digestive discomfort—and that dose varies by individual.

KEEP A FOOD JOURNAL

Track what, when, and where you eat, as well as how you feel before, during, and after. This heightens your awareness and helps you better understand—and reconsider—your food choices. Start journaling the week before any elimination diet, so you can identify any potential trigger foods.

GOLDEN RULE No.8

remember to stay hydrated

Water is crucial to our well-being: It makes up about 60 percent of our bodies, and every system depends on it. Water carries nutrients to cells, moistens membranes, cushions and protects joints and organs, regulates body temperature, keeps the digestive tract working smoothly, and helps flush out toxins and waste. The need to stay hydrated is a simple concept, yet there are plenty of questions—and some controversy—about just how to do so.

HOW MUCH IS ENOUGH?

The "eight glasses a day" rule may serve as a good rule of thumb, but there's no scientific evidence that this magic number improves health. Besides, some people need less, others more—especially when exercising, pregnant or breast-feeding, or suffering from an illness. Hydrate whenever you are thirsty, and check your urine: It should be light-colored (like lemonade), not dark yellow or amber (like apple juice); and you should feel the need to urinate at least once every two to four hours.

Extreme thirst, dry mouth, headache, fatigue, and irritability are early signs of mild dehydration, and drinking a glass of water should relieve the symptoms right away. Left unquenched for too long, however, dehydration can lead to more severe complications, including heatstroke and even seizures.

THE BEST SOURCES

Drinking water is still the best way to stay hydrated, but it's not the only one. Even tea and coffee contribute to your daily fluid intake (despite being mild diuretics), as do milk and juice. The fresh juices and smoothies on pages 116 to 117 are especially good hydrators.

What's on your plate counts, too: The IOM estimates that 20 percent of our water intake comes from food. Fresh produce can contain more than 85 percent water, plus it boasts fiber, antioxidants, and other essential nutrients. Top contenders include cucumbers, lettuces, celery, radishes, bell peppers, tomatoes, summer squash, spinach, carrots, cauliflower, and broccoli, as well as watermelon, berries, oranges and grapefruits, cantaloupe and honeydew, apples, and pears. Still other options include yogurt and even some cooked foods.

FRESH FROM THE TREE

Coconut water delivers many of the same electrolytes as bottled sports drinks, but none of the added sugars and additives. Buy unsweetened versions, or make your own: Remove the husk from a young green coconut, cut a circle around the top, and pry open. Sip through a straw or pour off into a glass. Mix it with chilled green tea for even more hydrating properties (plus antioxidants), or add a drizzle of honey for sweetness.

establish smart meal-planning habits

Rather than approach meals on an ad-hoc basis, consider this: If you take the hurry and unpredictability out of meal preparation, you'll be rewarded with a much more wholesome, nutritious, and flavorful meal.

SHOP BETTER

Start by streamlining your shopping to just one or two days each week: Fewer trips to the supermarket mean fewer opportunities to buy more than you need, or the wrong types of food. Try to shop on the weekend or whenever you aren't rushed for time (or hungry for dinner). You'll be more inclined to focus on what you are buying, and pay closer attention to nutritional information on the labels.

Whenever possible, shop at farmers' markets or greenmarkets, or sign up for your local Community Supported Agricultural (CSA) plan. You'll get the freshest seasonal produce—and discover new fruits and vegetables along the way.

STRATEGIZE

It's a good idea to plan your meals for the week, and to look for opportunities to make the most of the ingredients you have on hand, with the goal of not wasting anything. For example, if the salad you are making on Monday calls for half a bunch of scallions or basil, look for a soup or stir-fry to make later in the week that uses up the rest. Also, take inventory of your pantry at the beginning of each week and stock up on wholesome basics (including grains, legumes, onions, and other alliums) that serve as building blocks for healthy meals.

COOK ONCE, EAT TWICE

By all means take advantage of "big batch" cooking: Roasted vegetables can be incorporated into a salad, tossed with whole-grain pasta, or folded into omelets. Dried beans or legumes are always good make-ahead options (they can even be frozen in single servings), as are whole grains and breakfast favorites like granola and muesli.

know what you are buying

Understanding what grocery-store buzzwords mean—and what they don't mean—is essential for establishing good shopping habits. Here are some of the most common terms:

ORGANIC

Used for produce that is free of Genetically Modified Organisms (GMOs), grown without pesticides or synthetic herbicides, and not irradiated; for dairy, beef, and poultry, it means animals were given organic feed. "Certified organic" means production methods were verified by an independent inspector. There are three USDA-approved labels for packaged foods: "100 percent organic" products must include all organic ingredients, "organic" at least 95 percent, and "made with organic ingredients" at least 70 percent.

NATURAL

Refers to products made without artificial flavors or colors or synthetic substances, but the Food and Drug Administration (FDA) allows processed sweeteners (corn syrup, fructose, juice concentrates), "natural" flavors and colors (derived from natural sources but produced in a lab), and additives and preservatives.

FREE-RANGE

Indicates that an animal was raised with access to the outdoors. This claim is only regulated by the U.S. Department of Agriculture (USDA) for poultry chickens, not for egg-laying chickens or meat. Only five minutes of open-air access per day is enough to qualify. Cage-Free refers to eggs from hens that aren't confined to cages, whether or not they actually make it out to fresh air.

HORMONE-FREE

Means that no hormones were used during the production of the product. No organization verifies these claims beyond what is already required by the USDA, which prohibits the use of hormones on pork and poultry but allows certain ones for cows.

RAISED WITHOUT ANTIBIOTICS

Indicates that no antibiotics were used in the production of a meat or dairy product. The USDA doesn't use the term "antibiotic-free" because it considers it unprovable.

CERTIFIED HUMANE

Used for meat, dairy, and eggs to indicate that the animals were raised in humane conditions, with sufficient space and freedom to move, and were not subjected to artificial means to induce growth, such as for chickens.

SUGAR-FREE

A product that makes this claim (or "no added sugar") cannot contain added sugars. It can still have artificial chemical sweeteners, however, such as aspartame, Splenda, or saccharin, or sugar alcohols, such as sorbitol, xylitol, or maltitol, which can affect the digestive system adversely if consumed in large quantities.

GOLDEN RULE No.11

maintain a healthy perspective

It can be hard to know what you should be eating when there are so many fad diets and conflicting media headlines (carbohydrates are bad! carbohydrates are good!). But the age-old adage still holds sway: Everything in moderation, including moderation. So while this book promotes *focusing* on a whole-food, plant-based diet, it does not suggest that you can never eat those favorite foods (be they bacon, buttery mashed potatoes, or even ice cream) that don't fit in these categories.

THE RIGHT BALANCE

The goal is to balance your desire to be as healthy as you can be and to feel your best, with the overarching desire to also derive pleasure in what you eat. Because ultimately that's what food should do—nourish mind and body. And that varies by individual. For you, that may mean eating clean during the week and then indulging a bit over the weekend; for others, it might be more about trying to replace one or two meals a week with something healthier. Still others find total satisfaction in avoiding meat, dairy, sugar, gluten, and alcohol every day of the year. Again, it's about finding the right balance for you.

LIFESTYLE CHOICE

Keep in mind that when we feel deprived of something we really enjoy, many of us tend to rebel, and that's not conducive to a long-term commitment. The guilt that comes with the American diet has been shown time and again to be defeating, when the answer is simple: portion control and moderation.

Aim to form healthy habits, and a healthy relationship to food, without all the anxiety that often comes with deprivation diets. Once you learn to appreciate what food can do for you in terms of improving your health, you'll be more likely to make good choices, you'll begin to feel better, and you'll be motivated to continue until it's no longer a choice, it's a way of life.

KNOW YOUR NUTRIENTS

Arm yourself with the information you need, and you will be well on your way to making the healthiest choices.

More than just a means of nourishing your body and mind, food can also help to guard against disease and to strengthen your immunity. Certain foods can even function as medicine: They fortify the body with antioxidants and other essential nutrients, rid it of harmful toxins, and prevent inflammation, which can trigger disease. With 70 to 80 percent of the body's immune system located in the gut, the right foods can also provide the body with the nutrients necessary to promote a strong and healthy digestive system.

The glossaries that follow—photographs and descriptions of the most widely recognized super detoxifiers, antioxidant powerhouses, inflammation fighters, and digestive aids—highlight those foods with the strongest properties in their respective categories. Keep in mind that many plant-based foods possess multiple benefits: Antioxidant-rich berries are also potent anti-inflammatory agents, ginger has both detoxifying and digestive properties, and so on. Also, just because a food is missing from a glossary doesn't mean it's not a good source of those nutrients (most fruits and vegetables contribute vitamins and minerals and fiber). But by all means, for optimum health, prioritize the foods that are listed, keep them in ready supply, and put them in your regular meal rotation.

ALLERGY ALERT
Like with any type of food, certain allergies or intolerances can cause reactions that can counter any positive anti-inflammatory effects a food might have (see "Pay Attention to How You Feel," page 27). Check with your doctor or nutritionist if you think this might be the case.

super detoxifiers

Naturally cleansing foods contain properties that support the liver (the primary detoxifying organ), plus ample fiber to help flush out harmful toxins.

CELERY This alkalizing vegetable is known for its diuretic properties, which help rid the body of excess fluids and toxins. Its seeds cleanse the liver, thanks to their ability to reduce uric acid.

CAYENNE PEPPER Capsaicin, which gives peppers their fiery heat, helps stimulate the detoxification process by increasing blood flow. It also stimulates the sweat glands, another way the body filters out toxins.

WATERCRESS This peppery green helps energize cleansing enzymes in the liver, making it an excellent detoxifier.

CITRUS FRUITS Lemons, limes, and grapefruits are powerful detoxifiers thanks to the phytonutrient limonoid, which promotes the formation of enzymes in the liver that flush toxins. Red and pink grapefruits contain lycopene, which protects against prostate cancer.

SEA VEGETABLES Also called sea-weeds, sea vegetables such as nori, kelp, and kombu contain algin, which absorbs heavy metals and other toxins from the digestive tract. They also contain more kinds of minerals than any other food.

ALLIUMS Onions, leeks, shallots, garlic, and chives contain flavonoids that stimulate the production of glutathione, a potent antioxidant that encourages the elimination of toxins and carcinogens in the liver.

BEET High in antioxidants, this root vegetable contains betaine, a compound that encourages the liver to flush toxins. Beet fiber also helps increase the production of detoxifying enzymes in the liver.

ARTICHOKE Besides being high in fiber, this prickly thistle contains the powerful antioxidant silymarin, which boosts liver function. As a result, it is also a potent detoxifier.

AVOCADO This naturally creamy fruit is high in glutathione, a compound that supports liver detoxification. Plus, it has both soluble and insoluble fiber, which aid digestion and improve blood sugar and cholesterol levels.

DANDELION GREENS A potent diuretic, these liver-cleansing greens help enhance the flow of bile, essential for liver detoxification.

FENNEL Another natural diuretic, fennel helps remove toxic substances from the body. The mineral-rich seeds facilitate proper absorption of nutrients in the stomach and intestines.

CILANTRO Also known as fresh coriander, cilantro helps cleanse the body of toxic metals such as mercury, arsenic, and lead. It also possesses anti-bacterial and anticancer properties.

FLAXSEED The soluble and insoluble fiber in these tiny seeds promotes regu-larity, which helps eliminate toxins. They are also rich in heart-healthy omega-3 fatty acids.

BRASSICAS Members of this fam-ily promote the elimination of toxins thanks to their high content of gluco-sinolates, sulfur-containing compounds that are also responsible for their bitter flavors. Cabbage, brussels sprouts, and broccoli are particularly detoxifying.

KEY

1. Celery
2. Cayenne Pepper
3. Watercress
4. Clementine
5. Nori
6. Garlic
7. Lemon
8. Grapefruit
9. Artichoke
10. Avocado
11. Beet
12. Dandelion Greens
13. Onion
14. Fennel
15. Cilantro
16. Flaxseed
17. Cabbage

antioxidant powerhouses

These foods are flush with vitamins C and E, beta carotene, and flavonoids, which neutralize free radicals that contribute to the onset of aging and disease.

DARK BEANS Small red beans, pinto beans, and kidney beans are excellent sources of antioxidants, with small red beans topping the list.

DARK CHOCOLATE AND CACAO Dark chocolate (at least 70 percent cacao) and unsweetened cocoa powder are rich in antioxidants. Heating chocolate destroys some of its health-giving properties.

PECAN These tree nuts are rich in vitamin E, an antioxidant that helps prevent cell damage.

RED GRAPES For a powerful dose of antioxidants, choose red or purple grape varieties such as Concord over the less potent green variety.

APPLE Phytochemicals called polyphenols make apples a good source of antioxidants. But don't remove the skin—it contains substantially higher levels of antioxidants than the flesh.

PLUM The high vitamin C content and phenolic compounds in this fruit provide significant antioxidant protection.

EXTRA-VIRGIN OLIVE OIL This heart-healthy oil has strong concentrations of polyphenols, which have both antioxidant and anti-inflammatory properties.

BERRIES These fruits are among the highest in disease-fighting antioxidants. Their rich colors are the result of flavonoids, the phytochemicals that can counter cell damage.

WINTER SQUASH These gourds get their incredible antioxidant properties from beta-carotene and vitamin C.

CARROT Take a cue from their color: Carrots contain more carotenoids—antioxidants that help protect against certain cancers, heart disease, and cataracts—than any other vegetable. Beta-carotene is also converted in the body to vitamin A, which is essential for healthy skin and vision and helps support immunity.

SWEET POTATO These brightly colored roots are packed with the antioxidant beta-carotene, which the body converts to retinol, or vitamin A. They also have anti-inflammatory properties.

KIWI Loaded with vitamins C and E and lutein, this vine-growing fruit delivers a whopping dose of antioxidants, and has been shown to nourish the friendly bacteria in the gut.

COFFEE AND TEA These are full of flavonoids, plant-derived antioxidants that halt oxidative damage to cells and reduce the risk of heart disease. Contrary to popular opinion, coffee has more than tea.

CLOVE High levels of phenolic compounds give this spice antioxidant and anti-inflammatory properties.

SWEET CHERRIES Rich in quercetin, a powerful antioxidant that helps modulate inflammation and also acts as an antihistamine (thereby reducing the effects of allergies), this fruit also contains significant amounts of melatonin, which helps with insomnia.

DARK, LEAFY GREENS Rich in antioxidants and folate, these greens also help decrease inflammation—plus, their chlorophyll content supports the body's ability to detoxify.

KEY
1. Pinto Beans
2. Dark Chocolate
3. Small Red Beans
4. Pecans
5. Red Grapes
6. Apple
7. Plum
8. Extra-Virgin Olive Oil
9. Blackberries
10. Dumpling Squash
11. Carrot
12. Raspberries
13. Sweet Potato
14. Black Beans
15. Kiwi
16. Green Tea
17. Clove
18. Butternut Squash
19. Sweet Cherries
20. Kale
21. Blueberries
22. Cacao Powder

FREE RADICALS
These unstable oxygen molecules, which are linked to a host of chronic illnesses, cause oxidative stress in the body that can lead to inflammation. "Free radical damage is like rust in the inside of our bodies, in the cells themselves," explains Mark Hyman, M.D.

inflammation fighters

Omega-3s, vitamin E, and other potent compounds all help to prevent inflammation, thereby reducing the risk of cancer and heart disease, and soothing the aches and pains associated with arthritis.

WALNUTS These are one of the only foods that offer appreciable amounts of alpha-linolenic acid, an omega-3 fatty acid with heart-healthy benefits that reduces inflammation.

SPICES Natural healers, many spices contain anti-inflammatory properties. Turmeric contains compounds called curcuminoids that may help prevent Alzheimer's disease, joint inflammation, and carpal tunnel syndrome. Nutmeg, peppercorns, ginger, and cinnamon are other potent spices.

HERBS Many herbs, including rosemary, thyme, and oregano, offer strong antioxidant and anti-inflammatory properties. In addition, they possess antiviral, antifungal, and antimicrobial qualities, giving them an all-around exceptional nutritional value.

PAPAYA Significant amounts of vitamins A, C, and E in this tropical fruit reduce inflammation. The enzyme papain improves digestion.

COLD-WATER FISH Cold-water fish such as black cod, salmon, sardines, and anchovies are excellent sources of omega-3 fatty acids. Wild salmon's pink hue is the result of an abundance of carotenoids, which also have anti-inflammatory properties.

SHIITAKE MUSHROOMS These Asian mushrooms are nutritional champions. Antioxidants thioproline and ergothioneine attack free radicals and reduce inflammation. The carbohydrate lentinan keeps the immune system strong.

BOK CHOY This variety of cabbage boasts a high concentration of beta-carotene and vitamin A, which have potent anti-inflammatory and anti-cancer effects.

KEY
1. Walnuts
2. Black Peppercorns
3. Rosemary
4. Thyme
5. Papaya
6. Sardines
7. Nutmeg
8. Shiitake Mushrooms
9. Cinnamon
10. Salmon
11. Bok Choy

digestive aids

Loaded with beneficial bacteria and fiber, these foods keep the digestive system running smoothly.

ALMONDS High in vitamin E, healthy fats, and other minerals, almonds also have prebiotic benefits, which help feed the good bacteria.

ASPARAGUS A member of the lily family, asparagus contains inulin, a carbohydrate that helps promote the growth of healthy bacteria in the large intestine. Asparagus is also high in fiber, which adds to its digestive benefits.

COCONUT Coconut and coconut oil contain lauric acid, a medium chain triglyceride (MCT) that is helpful for digestive healing.

FERMENTED DAIRY Kefir, a fermented milk drink (the name means "good feeling"), and yogurt contain live and active cultures that may help maintain the health of the digestive tract, boost the immune system, prevent yeast infections, and lower cholesterol.

FERMENTED VEGETABLES Kimchi, sauerkraut, and other fermented vegetables are excellent sources of the healthy bacteria lactobacilli, which aid digestion. This good bacteria also helps control appetite by lowering blood-sugar levels.

FLAXSEED In addition to being used as a detoxifier (see page 39), these seeds are used to improve digestive health and relieve constipation. Mix a tablespoon of freshly ground flaxseed into breakfast cereals, yogurt, or baked goods.

GINGER This popular digestive tonic, appetite stimulant, and anti-nausea treatment contains gingerols and shogaols, which help neutralize stomach acids.

HONEY Thanks to its antiseptic properties, raw honey relieves acidity and neutralizes gas, making it an excellent stomach soother. Raw local honey may also help with allergies.

LEGUMES This class of vegetables, which includes a variety of beans, peas, and lentils, contains both soluble and insoluble fibers, which help promote regularity. If legumes aren't already part of your diet, be sure to introduce them gradually in order to avoid any excess gas or bloating.

MINT This herb contains volatile oils that effectively relax the stomach muscles and relieve gas.

MISO Made by fermenting a mixture of soybeans, barley, brown rice, and other grains with a fungus called *Aspergillus oryzae*, this Asian paste is a probiotic food that helps support the digestive system by adding beneficial bacteria to the existing intestinal colonies.

TURMERIC This Indian spice contains curcumin, a powerful antioxidant that stimulates bile production and, as a result, aids the digestive process.

WHOLE GRAINS Whole grains such as brown rice, oats, and farro are packed with insoluble fiber, which aids the digestive process by softening the stool and adding bulk. Stick to gluten-free grains if you have gluten sensitivities.

KEY

1. Mint
2. Miso
3. Flaxseed
4. Green Lentils
5. Almonds
6. Red Lentils
7. Ginger
8. Oats
9. Yogurt
10. Turmeric
11. Honey
12. Asparagus
13. Coconut
14. Farro
15. Kimchi

RESTOCK YOUR PANTRY

The first step toward cooking clean food is to fill your pantry with the foundations of a plant-based diet: whole grains, beans and other legumes, and healthy fats, plus some natural flavor enhancers. Making some nutritious substitutions can also help (see chart, opposite).

smart swaps

Replace a few items with healthier options—choosing quinoa over couscous and olive oil instead of vegetable oil—as a good way to ease into a cleaner diet. Start with the ones below, then read on for other suggestions.

REPLACE THIS → WITH THIS

SOUR CREAM → YOGURT
Cup for cup, whole-milk yogurt has less than half the calories and one third the total fat of sour cream. Use it in dips and dressings and to top soups.

CREAM CHEESE → ALMOND BUTTER
With more fiber, calcium, and vitamin E, plus heart-healthy fat, almond butter makes a great alternative to cream cheese on toast and sandwiches.

MAYONNAISE → AVOCADO
Looking for something rich and creamy to spread on a sandwich? Try mashed avocado. Per tablespoon, this mild, buttery fruit has about half the fat (and mostly the "good" kind) plus ample fiber.

WHITE POTATO → SWEET POTATO
Baked, roasted, or mashed, sweet potatoes offer all the comfort-food satisfaction of white potatoes—but with much more nutrition.

ICEBERG LETTUCE → ROMAINE LETTUCE
Iceberg lettuce is no nutritional star, but it adds nice crunch to salads, tacos, and sandwiches. Romaine is just as crunchy, but offers more fiber and other nutrients.

MILK CHOCOLATE → DARK CHOCOLATE
Dark chocolate gets its signature bitter flavor from flavonoids, heart-protecting antioxidants that milk chocolate contains in short supply.

CROUTONS → WALNUTS
Like croutons, walnuts add heft and texture to salads. But thanks to their protein, fiber, and healthy fat, they also add long-lasting energy.

BUTTON MUSHROOMS → SHIITAKE MUSHROOMS
Mushrooms provide more nutrients than they get credit for, but shiitakes stand out for their combination of great flavor and cancer-fighting properties.

NOTE
This doesn't mean button mushrooms or white potatoes are "bad" for you (they both appear in recipes in this book). It's just that, whenever possible, you should make the healthier option your default one.

whole grains

On average, Americans eat fewer than one serving of whole grains per day and far too many refined grains. The problem may be that many of us don't know what constitutes a "whole grain." Here's a good place to start: Eating whole grains in their natural state is generally better than getting your quota from grain-based products like bread or pasta, even when these products are made from whole-grain or whole-wheat flour (i.e., refined grains; see "About Food Labels," opposite).

whole vs. refined

Although both types of grains—whole and refined—are good sources of carbohydrates and are low in fat, whole grains are better sources of fiber and much-needed nutrients like selenium, potassium, and magnesium. That's because whole grains contain all three parts of a grain: the bran, the endosperm, and the germ. The bran encompasses dietary fiber, a source of B vitamins, and certain trace minerals. The germ is the embryo of the seed, which has B vitamins and vitamin E, essential fatty acids, phytonutrients, and unsaturated fats. The endosperm provides the germ's food supply and includes proteins, B vitamins, and most of the grain's calories, in the form of starch. The slow-to-digest carbohydrates of whole grains help to control blood sugar. But the starch in refined flours is pulverized, stripping it of its fibrous bran hull and oil-rich germ to create a form that's rapidly digested.

health benefits

There's a strong body of evidence to support the many positive health effects of fiber-rich whole grains. They've been shown to lower total and LDL ("bad") cholesterol and triglycerides and to regulate insulin, which can help reduce the risk of cardiovascular disease. Eating just two or three servings of whole grains a day has been linked to a 30 percent lower risk of having a heart attack or dying from heart disease. A diet rich in whole grains may also decrease your odds of developing type 2 diabetes: A study of 161,737 women combined with data from six cohort studies found that those who averaged two to three servings a day of whole grains had a more than 20 percent lower risk of developing type 2 diabetes than those who consumed less. Plus, according to *American Journal of Clinical Nutrition,* people who consumed the most whole grains were significantly less likely to die from inflammation-related diseases over a 17-year period.

what to buy

Popular whole grains such as rice, oats, and wheat tend to overshadow other flavorful choices that also happen to be more nutritious. Consider less-familiar options such as farro and millet as a great way to add more grains to your diet, without sacrificing taste or variety. Whenever possible, buy whole grains in bulk from a natural food market or health food store, and make sure the store has a high turnover so its supply is frequently replenished. You can also purchase whole grains in bulk online.

ABOUT FOOD LABELS
Not all whole grains are created equal. Be wary of labels that say "made with whole grains" as these products may be made with refined grains. Terms such as "multigrain," "cracked wheat," "100 percent wheat," "whole-grain flour," "seven grain," and "stone-ground" do not mean the same thing as whole grain. This is especially true for bread. Select dense, chewy varieties with whole or cracked grains that are visible and listed as their first ingredient, and with at least 2 grams of fiber per serving.

types of whole grains

AMARANTH Once held sacred by the Aztecs, amaranth is actually a small herb seed, not a cereal grain. It is gluten-free and rich in protein and fiber, and has a slightly peppery taste. Amaranth can be baked into muffins, or toasted with other grains for granola.

BARLEY Known for its chewiness and mild sweetness, barley contains the highest source of beta-glucans, which help to lower cholesterol. Whole, hulled barley is called Scotch or pot barley; this can be soaked overnight to reduce the cooking time. Pearl barley, which is more widely available, has had the bran layer (and some nutrients) removed. Enjoy barley as a warm breakfast cereal, or use it to bulk up soups and stews.

BROWN RICE Unlike white rice, brown rice has its bran and germ intact, so it has more vitamins and fiber, as well as a stronger flavor and chewier texture. The shorter the grain, the more starchy it will be; the size has no affect on nutritional quality. Short-grain brown rice works well in Asian-style dishes, while long-grain brown rice is a good all-purpose option in side dishes and soups.

BUCKWHEAT Most buckwheat is used to feed animals and improve crop soil. The rest is usually made into flour. It is popular in Eastern European cooking. In Japan and Korea, buckwheat noodles, or soba, are a staple. Soba is sometimes made with a combination of wheat and buckwheat; read the label if you are avoiding or limiting your gluten intake.

BULGUR Sometimes referred to as cracked wheat, bulgur is ground after it's been boiled, but it is still considered a whole grain. During the boiling process, the endosperm absorbs the nutrients from the bran layers—keeping the grain relatively intact. Use bulgur in salads such as tabbouleh.

FARRO Italian for emmer wheat, farro is intensely flavorful and has a high concentration of B vitamins. Farro is only considered a whole grain when the bran is still partially intact (labeled "semi-perlato"); it's not a whole grain when the bran is removed (labeled "pearl" or "perlato"). Farro can be used in place of pasta in salads, or it can be prepared risotto-style.

KAMUT Although kamut (pronounced kah-MOOT) is related to durum wheat, many people who are gluten intolerant can eat it. This ancient grain, otherwise known as khorasan, is an excellent source of protein, vitamins, and minerals; it has a rich, buttery flavor and pleasant, chewy texture. Kamut is good in pilafs and grain salads.

MILLET The benefits of millet's superior protein once made it a staple in Africa, China, and India, before rice became the principal grain. Millet is loaded with B vitamins and is gluten-free. Use it in granola, muesli, hot cereals, vegetable burgers, and pilafs.

OATS Hulled whole oats (called groats) are the most basic form of oats, and they can be cooked like other grains to make hearty breakfast cereals or savory dishes. Rolled ("old-fashioned") oats are groats that have been flattened for faster cooking; steel-cut oats are groats that have been cut with steel blades instead of rolled. Oats in nearly all their forms (except instant or quick-cooking) have comparable nutritional profiles.

QUINOA Technically a grain-like seed, quinoa (pronounced KEEN-wah) is gluten-free and high in fiber, and it has all nine essential amino acids that make a complete protein. It has a subtle, sweet, nutty taste and can be cooked into pilafs, grain salads, and vegetable burgers.

SPELT This sweet, full-flavored heirloom variety of wheat is higher in protein than regular wheat, and it can be tolerated by some people with gluten sensitivities. It has a similar texture to farro and can be prepared in much the same manner.

WHEAT BERRIES These are the whole unprocessed wheat kernels, which are high in protein and fiber and a good source of other nutrients and antioxidants. Wheat berries have a nutty flavor and chewy texture that works well in pilafs and salads. For plumper grains, you can soak the berries for several hours before cooking, if desired.

cooking whole grains

The most common way to cook whole grains is by the absorption method: Bring water (or stock), grains, and salt (if desired) to a boil; simmer, covered, until the grains are tender and the water has been absorbed, then let stand ten minutes before fluffing with a fork. Cooking times will vary slightly, depending on how chewy or tender a texture you prefer. Toasting the grains in the pan before adding the water will yield a nuttier flavor. The chart below is for one cup of grains, which typically yields up to four servings.

ALTERNATIVE METHOD
You can also cook some grains—including kamut, spelt, oat groats, and wheat berries—as you would pasta, in ample water to cover: Bring grains, water, and salt (if desired) to a boil, then reduce heat and simmer until grains reach the desired texture. Drain in a sieve (you will lose a little flavor and nutrition with the water).

TYPE OF GRAIN (1 CUP)	CUPS OF WATER	COOKING MINUTES
AMARANTH	2	20
BARLEY (HULLED)	3	35–40
BROWN RICE	3	35–50
BUCKWHEAT	2	15
BULGUR	2	20
FARRO	3	30–35
KAMUT	3	45–60
MILLET	2	30–35
OATS (HULLED)	1	60
QUINOA	2	15
SPELT	3	45
WHEAT BERRIES	1	30–40

pasta

Despite being a type of refined grain, pasta can still be part of a clean food diet. It has a relatively low glycemic index, meaning it won't cause spikes in blood sugar and insulin the way that many other products made from flour do. This is partly because of pasta's density, which causes it to be more slowly digested than other starches. Also, most pasta is made from semolina flour, derived from nutrient-rich durum wheat, making it higher in protein and lower in starch than all-purpose flour.

The problem with pasta stems from the way Americans tend to eat it—in portions that are too large and covered with creamy or other less-than-healthful sauces. Instead, limit yourself to four ounces of pasta per serving, no more than two to three times a week, and mix it with plenty of lean proteins, like beans and seafood, and vegetables. Experiment with Asian-style noodle dishes, which are typically well balanced. And cook pasta just until al dente, which will have an even lower glycemic index than pasta cooked until soft. It's also worth exploring the following alternatives to traditional pasta; they have improved in taste and texture over previous versions.

WHOLE-GRAIN PASTAS

Ounce per ounce, pasta made from whole wheat, spelt, farro, and kamut offers more fiber (about 19 grams per 4 ounces), nutrients, and protein than semolina pasta. Whole-wheat and kamut pastas also provide antioxidants. Soba, or buckwheat, noodles offer good-quality protein; those that are 100 percent buckwheat (with no added wheat) are also gluten-free.

GLUTEN-FREE PASTAS

Try whole-grain pasta made from brown rice, millet, quinoa, lentils, or beans (black or mung), which have more fiber and nutrients—and better texture and flavor—than pasta made from corn or white rice. When cooking, check the pot a few minutes before the directions suggest, to keep them from turning mushy; rinsing under cold water to stop the cooking helps, too.

legumes

Hearty, healthy legumes—beans, lentils, and peas—are the best sources of plant protein on earth. Good news for anyone wanting to cut back on, or cut out entirely, animal-based proteins. Rich in soluble and insoluble fiber, beans are good sources of low-glycemic carbohydrates, which makes them more slowly digested and less likely to raise blood sugar. Plus, they are packed with vitamins, minerals, and other nutrients. Legumes are also versatile and come in many varieties, making it easy to get the recommended one or two half-cup servings every day.

health benefits

Besides protein, beans and other legumes are packed with nutrients such as folate, potassium, magnesium, copper, iron, and zinc. They're also high in both soluble and insoluble fiber—one half-cup serving of cooked beans provides more than seven grams, a quarter of the recommended daily value—so they are effective at reducing total cholesterol and regulating blood sugar and insulin. New research suggests that a diet rich in legumes may be particularly beneficial to those suffering from type 2 diabetes. According to a report published in the November 2012 issue of *Archives of Internal Medicine*, patients who ate a bean-rich diet (at least 1 cup per day) lowered their blood-sugar levels and reduced their risk of cardiovascular disease through lowered blood pressure. Researchers have also found a reduced risk of cancer in people who ate legumes two or more times a week, possibly due to the foods' protective phytochemicals.

A NOTE ABOUT CANNED BEANS
Canned beans are easy to use and shelf stable, but they can be high in sodium. Rinse well before using to lower the sodium (to about a third of the original amount) and to remove indigestible starches found in the liquid. Better yet, buy canned beans labeled "low sodium" or "no sodium added." Can linings may also contain the potentially harmful chemical bisphenol A (BPA), so look for brands that are BPA-free (check the label).

preparing legumes

Dried beans cost less, offer greater variety, give more control over sodium intake, and can be cooked in big batches and kept on hand for quick additions to meals. To ensure freshness, always buy dried beans and legumes from a source with a high turnover; older ones will be tougher and take longer to cook.

RINSING AND SOAKING

All legumes should be picked over for dirt and pebbles and rinsed well with cold water. Most dried beans require soaking to soften before cooking. Lentils, black-eyed peas, and split peas do not. Place beans in a bowl, and cover with three times their volume of water; soak, refrigerated, at least 4 hours and up to 24 hours. Or do a quick soak: Place beans in a pot, and add water to cover by 3 inches. Bring to a boil, and continue to boil for 2 minutes. Cover, remove from heat, and let sit for 1 hour before proceeding.

COOKING

Place dried beans or other legumes in a pot with their soaking liquid or fresh water to cover by 2 inches; add herbs, garlic, and other aromatics, if desired. Bring to a boil, and then reduce heat and simmer gently, stirring occasionally, 20 to 30 minutes for lentils, about 45 minutes for split peas and black-eyed peas, and up to 2 hours for most beans. Cooking time depends on the age of the beans, so taste them periodically to test. When done, they should be soft throughout but still retain their shape. If they are the least bit crunchy, they are not fully cooked. Refrigerate legumes, in their cooking liquid, for 3 to 5 days; let cool completely before storing.

COOKING BEANS

If you experience gas or bloating after eating beans, try any of the following: Discard the soaking liquid (and with it some of the indigestible starches) before cooking. Add a piece of kombu (seaweed) to the cooking water before simmering; it will eventually dissolve without affecting taste or texture. Or cook the beans with digestion-supporting herbs or spices like fennel seeds, ginger, and asafoetida.

SUGGESTED USES

Add cooked legumes to soups, stews, or salads, or puree them to make dips or sandwich spreads. Try experimenting: Prepare hummus with pureed edamame; make Indian dal with mung beans; or change up the rice-and-bean combination with different types of both.

types of legumes

AZUKI BEANS These quick-cooking, high-protein, small red beans have a sweet, nutty flavor and contain easily digestible sugars. Try adding them to vegetarian chili or Asian dishes.

BLACK BEANS A relative of the kidney bean, black beans have the most antioxidant activity of all beans; the blacker the bean, the greater the anthocyanin content, which helps stave off heart disease. Black beans have a rich meatiness that pairs well with Latin American flavors.

BLACK-EYED PEAS Besides being a good source of fiber and plant protein, black-eyed peas are high in zinc, an essential trace mineral that also has antioxidant properties. They do not require presoaking and can be cooked in water or broth until tender.

CHICKPEAS Also known as garbanzo beans, chickpeas originated in the Middle East and remain a popular staple in its cuisine, as well as in Indian and Italian cooking. They have been shown to significantly lower cholesterol when added to a healthy diet.

EDAMAME Simply green soybeans harvested before reaching maturity, edamame provide more protein than all other beans, and they contain all the essential amino acids, making them as complete a protein as meat. Boil the beans in their pods, and eat as a snack; or add the shelled beans to salads and stir-fries. Frozen edamame is a fine substitute for fresh, which can be hard to find in the United States.

FAVA BEANS In spring to early summer, look for fresh fava beans, which are creamy, full-bodied, and slightly sweet. To peel them, first remove the beans from their shells and blanch in boiling water for 2 minutes; plunge into an ice-water bath until cool, then pop out of skin. Dried fava beans are also available, though not as readily as other beans.

KIDNEY BEANS Sold by color, ranging from white (called cannellini) to dark red, kidney beans are shaped like the namesake organ. Thanks to their dark skins, red kidney beans have almost as much antioxidant power as wild blueberries.

LENTILS These legumes are available in a rainbow of colors and have a pleasantly earthy flavor. Because they are an important source of iron, lentils make a great alternative to red meat. Lentils cook relatively quickly, so choose dried; canned lentils can be quite mushy.

LIMA BEANS These starchy beans sometimes show up fresh at farmers' markets, but you are more likely to find them dried, frozen (our recommendation), or canned at the grocery store. Fordhook limas also go by the name "butter beans," and they taste exactly as they sound.

MUNG BEANS These tiny beans sprout readily, cook quickly, and are easily digestible. They work particularly well in Asian dishes.

NAVY BEANS The tender, potato-like quality of these small beans made them a staple of the U.S. Navy (hence the name). Navy beans are an excellent source of manganese and copper, both essential in helping to rid the body of free radicals.

PINTO BEANS Pinkish brown with splotches of color, pinto beans are the most highly consumed dried bean in the United States. Research suggests that eating pinto beans regularly appears to lower both total and LDL ("bad") cholesterol. Pintos are a classic ingredient in Mexican dishes and stews such as chili. They also contain more total dietary fiber than most other beans and legumes.

SPLIT PEAS Made by steaming whole field peas to remove their skins, then splitting them so they cook faster, split peas are a no-soak alternative to other legumes. The green variety has a brighter flavor than the yellow. Besides being used in the classic soup, split peas are used to make Indian dal and stews.

healthy fats

A NOTE ABOUT DAIRY PRODUCTS Opinions vary on which is better for you: whole milk and products made from whole milk, because they are the least processed, or low-fat varieties, because they help you avoid getting too much saturated fat. Many nutritionists now suggest that the higher percentage of nutrients (and the richer taste) in full-fat dairy products makes them a better choice, as long as they are consumed in moderation.

Despite all the news about the health risks of a fatty diet, it's important to keep in mind that we all need at least some fat to survive. Our bodies need fat for energy, for vitamin absorption, for healthy hair and skin, and for fueling our metabolism, among other essential functions. Plus, fat carries flavor, and without it our food just wouldn't taste as good. The key to good health is to get the right type of fat, and in the right amount (too little of the good kind can be almost as detrimental as too much of the bad).

"good" vs. "bad" fats

Indeed, it's the type of fats you include in your diet that has the largest impact on your health. Some fats—such as saturated fat in red meat—are thought to raise cholesterol and increase your chances of developing heart disease. But others, like monounsaturated fats in extra-virgin olive oil and omega-3 fatty acids in cold-water fish like salmon, are vital to protecting the heart; omega-3s also help maintain optimum cognitive functioning. Many nutritionists recommend that beneficial fats should compose as much as 35 percent of a day's total calories.

"bad" fats

SATURATED FAT
Diets high in saturated fat may lead to increased LDL ("bad") cholesterol and a greater risk of heart disease. The main culprits are red meat and poultry (mostly the skin). Limit the amounts of these foods in your diet.

TRANS FATS
These dangerous fats are found in many processed foods, especially commercially made baked goods. They reduce HDL ("good") cholesterol, raise LDL cholesterol, and increase triglycerides (blood fats), while also promoting chronic inflammation, diabetes, and different forms of cancer. Avoid products with vegetable shortening, hydrogenated fats, or partially hydrogenated fats. Note that products claiming to have "no trans fats" can still contain 0.5 grams per serving.

"good" fats

MONOUNSATURATED FAT
Vegetable oils such as extra-virgin olive oil and expeller-pressed canola oil contain high percentages of monounsaturated fats that lower LDL cholesterol levels without affecting HDL levels, making them a better choice than oils containing polyunsaturated fats (PUFAs), which lower both LDL and HDL. See page 58 for other good sources of monounsaturated fats.

POLYUNSATURATED FATS
Omega-3 and -6 fatty acids are essential for human health, and the only way to get them is through your diet. The problem is that most Americans get too many omega-6 fatty acids, or polyunsaturated fats (PUFAs), and not enough omega-3s, or monounsaturated fats, and this may increase the risk of heart disease, cancer, Alzheimer's disease, and other inflammatory conditions. But PUFAs can still be part of a healthy diet—and can help reduce cholesterol levels and lower the risk of heart disease—when consumed in moderation and when used to replace saturated fats.

OMEGA-3 FATTY ACIDS
There are three types of omega-3 fatty acids: alpha-linolenic acid (LNA), eicosapentaenoic acid (EPA), and docosahexaenoic acid (DHA). LNA is derived mostly from plant sources, such as flaxseed and walnuts, whereas EPA and DHA are found in oily fish, such as salmon, sardines, and anchovies. Omega-3 fatty acids protect the heart by improving the ratio of HDL to LDL cholesterol and reducing inflammation, while also playing a role in the development of the brain and cognitive function.

Although natural sources are still considered the best way of getting the recommended supply of these essential fatty acids, they can also be found in products enriched with omega-3s, including orange juice, eggs, cereals, and pastas, as well as milk, yogurt, and cheese. Check the label for the types and amounts.

A NOTE ABOUT SAFFLOWER OIL
Canola oil and safflower oil are the types of vegetable oils we use in the recipes in this book for high-heat cooking. Unlike the regular variety of safflower oil, which contains mostly polyunsaturated fats (or PUFAs), those labeled "high-oleic" must have a minimum of 75 percent monounsaturated fat, in the form of omega-9 fatty acids. Always choose this type for cooking.

OMEGA-3 SUPPLEMENTS
If you don't eat fish (or take fish-oil capsules), consider supplementing your diet with algae oil, such as one sourced from Schizochytrium. "The DHA content in cold-water fish is due to their consumption of algae," says Cathy Wong, a licensed naturopathic doctor, who also recommends taking Echium oil, a plant oil that contains stearidonic acid, which the body converts to EPA.

types of healthy ("good") fats

AVOCADOS Half an avocado contains about 10 grams of fat—the majority monounsaturated—and only 160 calories; it also provides almost 7 grams of fiber, one third of the daily requirement, making it a nutrient-dense source of energy. Avocados are also incredibly versatile: Add to smoothies, dips and spreads (beyond guacamole), soups, salads, tacos, sandwiches, even pudding (see recipe, page 301). Or just snack on one with a little extra-virgin olive oil drizzled over it (for even more heart-healthy fat).

COOKING OILS Extra-virgin olive oil is still the gold standard for having the highest level of heart-healthy monounsaturated fats, and, unlike regular olive oil, is mechanically extracted without chemicals or added heat so it retains the most nutrients. Make this your all-purpose oil for preparing vinaigrettes, cooking in parchment, and roasting vegetables, fish, and other foods. Look for "cold-pressed" olive oils, which have been extracted in a heat-controlled environment to preserve their flavor, aroma, and nutrients.

Use heart-healthy oils with higher smoke points for higher-heat cooking. Canola oil has more omega-3s than other vegetable oils. High-oleic safflower oil is another good option for sautéing, as is grapeseed oil (but only in moderation since it contains PUFAs). Look for expeller-pressed varieties of these oils, which are

extracted without the use of harsh chemicals and will retain more nutrients. Peanut oil is another good option; high in monounsaturated fats, it also contains the heart-friendly phytochemical resveratrol, plus antioxidants that may help prevent breast cancer and other cancers.

Oil from the coconut palm tree has long been scorned for its high saturated content, and the American Heart Association recommends avoiding it. But emerging research suggests that coconut oil may actually safeguard the heart and help spur weight loss. The nutty, slightly sweet flavor is especially good for stir-frying, sautéing, and roasting vegetables, fish, and poultry. Make sure to buy only organic unrefined (often labeled "virgin" or "extra-virgin") coconut oil.

NUTS Nutrient-rich nuts are low in saturated fat yet high in good-for-you mono- and polyunsaturated fats, and are also among the best sources of phytosterols, which block the absorption of cholesterol, as well as other antioxidants (see page 41). Walnuts are the only nuts, and one of only a few foods (including walnut oil), to contain the omega-3 fatty acid alpha-lipoic acid (ALA). Cashews contain less fat than most other nuts, and a good percentage of it is oleic acid, the same monounsaturated fat found in olive oil. Almonds contain monounsaturated and polyunsaturated fats that help lower LDL ("bad") cholesterol. Pistachios are another good source of healthy

fats, plus they are high in antioxidants and potassium.

Studies have shown that eating a handful of nuts a day at least four times a week can lower the risk of heart disease. Besides making a handy snack, nuts can be incorporated into sweet and savory dishes, including granola, muesli, and salads. Or chop them and use in place of breadcrumbs for coating fish fillets or chicken cutlets.

OILY FISH The so-called oily cold-water fish are hands down the best source of omega-3 fatty acids, especially EPA and DHA. Of all the fish high in omega-3 fatty acids, these have the least contamination from mercury and PCBs according to the Environmental Defense Fund: wild Alaskan salmon, farmed rainbow trout, Atlantic mackerel, Alaskan or Canadian sablefish (black cod), and canned sardines and anchovies. Canned chunk light tuna (not albacore) is another option; because of its moderate levels of mercury, it is best eaten in moderation (no more than six servings per month). All of these types of fish are sustainably caught.

flavor enhancers

Just because you're cutting back on certain foods doesn't mean you have to cut back on flavor. Here are some healthful and delicious ways to liven up your meals.

ANCHOVIES Rich in omega-3s, these tiny fish add depth to vinaigrettes (see right), marinades, sauces, and sautéed vegetables. Look for jars of salt-packed fillets, which when rinsed will actually taste less salty, or those packed in extra-virgin olive oil.

CITRUS A fresh squeeze of lemon or lime adds just the right amount of acidity to round out most any dish, savory or sweet. The grated zest is equally flavorful.

DRIED PEPPERS Red-pepper flakes and ground dried chile peppers, add a nice kick. Incorporate them into all sorts of savory dishes, or sprinkle them over a snack of avocado and lime juice.

FINISHING OILS Nut and seed oils—walnut, hazelnut, avocado, and pumpkin—break down quickly when heated, so it's best not to cook with them; drizzle them over finished dishes instead.

FISH SAUCE A staple of Southeast Asian cooking, this fermented sauce is a good source of protein and B vitamins when used in moderation (it's high in sodium). Look for an all-natural, first-press fish sauce without added water, preservatives, or MSG, which are often found in second- and third-grade varieties.

FRESH HERBS Aim to include fresh varieties of herbs in every meal. They have many health benefits (see "Inflammation Fighters," page 43) and are a delicious way to enhance any dish.

GROUND SEEDS Grind seeds like flax, sunflower, and pumpkin seeds in a spice grinder or clean coffee mill, then sprinkle over everything from salads to breakfast porridges.

MISO This protein-rich fermented soybean paste imparts a savory taste the Japanese call umami (also called "the fifth flavor"). It comes in three varieties: shiro (white), aka (red), and awase (mixed). We prefer the mild taste of shiro.

NORI SPRINKLES These have higher levels of minerals than sheet nori, making them a nutritious addition to many savory dishes. Sprinkle over soups and salads, or incorporate into sauces, dressings, and dips.

SALT It's hard to think of any dish—even a dessert—that isn't improved by a sprinkle of salt. Opt for sea salts such as sel gris, fleur de sel, flake salt (such as Maldon), and Hawaiian sea salt. Himalayan salt is particularly rich in minerals and is believed to be one of the least processed salts available.

TOMATO PASTE Boost the flavor of savory dishes with this concentrated tomato puree. For an even richer flavor, cook it in olive oil until deep red and caramelized. Freeze leftover tomato paste in ice-cube trays for later use (transfer to resealable bags once firm).

VINEGAR Keep an assortment on hand to brighten virtually all manner of savory dishes. Varieties include: red wine, white wine, sherry, balsamic, apple cider, and rice vinegar.

OMEGA-3 VINAIGRETTE Whisk together 18 oil-packed sliced anchovies, $\frac{1}{3}$ cup extra-virgin olive oil, ¼ cup chopped fresh flat-leaf parsley leaves, 3 tablespoons fresh lemon juice, 2 teaspoons finely grated lemon zest, 2 teaspoons chopped shallots, and ½ teaspoon freshly ground pepper.

DETOX YOUR MIND AND BODY

The following 3-Day and 21-Day Action Plans are about cleaning the slate. Rest assured: Neither one is about anything as extreme as fasting. Instead, each plan is based on a wholesome and delicious mix of juices, smoothies, soups, salads, snacks, and lean proteins.

No matter which action plan you choose, these tips and strategies (and the ones on the following pages) will help you make the most of your cleanse. For best results, ease up on the "six to skip" the week before you begin.

how it works

SET GOALS Before the challenge, start a food journal, writing down five things that the detox means to you and what you hope to achieve. Use it to track what, when, and where you eat, as well as how you feel. Referencing this will heighten your awareness and help keep goals in sight if your enthusiasm ever flags.

DEVISE A STRATEGY Both plans include plenty of make-ahead and big-batch recipes, so prepping your meals should be quicker and easier. This means you'll always have a selection of leftovers in the refrigerator for other days.

MAKE IT YOUR OWN Feel free to improvise meals instead of following the preapproved menu plans; when choosing other recipes in this book, follow the ingredient guidelines ("What's on the Menu," page 64) for each week of the 21-Day Action Plan.

BUILD IN VARIETY Snacks are a way to change up your daily menu and add extra fiber and nutrients. Choose two snacks each day (see "Reboot," page 109). If you're too pressed for time, grab some nuts and fruit. Aim for around one ounce of nuts and two pieces of fruit a day. Be sure to space out your meals (including snacks), leaving a couple hours between each. And remember: Snack only when you're hungry.

six to skip

1. PROCESSED FOODS Too many unhealthy, refined ingredients and additives will weigh down your body. This goes for processed beverages, too (see "Golden Rule No. 1," page 14).

2. ADDED SUGARS White cane sugar and high fructose corn syrup are highly addictive and suppress the immune system. Reset your palate so that less cloying foods satisfy cravings. (Honey is okay in small amounts.)

3. DAIRY Digestive upset, diarrhea, heartburn, and chronic ear and sinus infections are all linked to this common allergen. Even if you're not allergic to dairy, omitting it from your diet during a cleanse helps give your digestion a break.

4. GLUTEN Found in wheat and other grains, this protein is difficult for many people to digest. Under-the-radar sensitivities can cause reactions as varied as brain fog and bloating.

5. ALCOHOL Particularly burdensome, alcohol enters the bloodstream and heads straight for the liver, where harmful free radicals are generated as it metabolizes.

6. COFFEE Life without this stimulant may reveal that you're seriously fatigued. Offset headaches by switching to black or green tea a week before the detox.

IN GOOD COMPANY It's easier to stay the course when you have the support of your friends, family, and colleagues. Enlist one (or two) of them to join; you can even take turns preparing the recipes.

SEE YOUR DOCTOR Before beginning this or any other program, take stock of your overall health. If you have any chronic and/or serious health condition, cleanse only under a doctor's supervision; even if you don't have a health condition, consulting a doctor is a good idea.

3-day action plan

Ready for a quick reboot? In just seventy-two hours, you can jump-start your way to a healthier body. "Nutrients found in colorful plant foods drive the process of liver detoxification," says Kathie Madonna Swift, R.D.N., an integrative medical nutritionist. These dishes give your digestive system a rest from processed foods and common allergens (see "Six to Skip," page 61). Loading up on fibrous fruits and vegetables helps remove toxins, which are eliminated by binding to fiber. Skip your morning coffee and evening glass of wine (both overwork the liver, the organ we're aiming to support); opt for water or herbal tea instead.

GET SOME SLEEP
Be sure to get at least seven and a half hours of sleep each night during this and any other detox program. You deserve it (and you need it for cleanse commitment).

EASY DOES IT

This mini detox is based on a streamlined menu of "big-batch" meals so that you can front-load all the work. Yes, you'll be having the same breakfast, lunch, and dinner during the cleanse, but three days of clean eating "is just the boost your body needs to support digestion and detoxification and to eliminate unwanted cravings," says Swift.

TUNE OUT
As much as possible, take a media fast: Curtail time spent surfing the Web, watching television, and texting and e-mailing, to give your mind a much-needed break, too.

TUNE IN
Focus on how you feel by building reflective downtime into your day, whether that's meditating, writing in a journal, or taking a walk in nature.

ICONS
- VEGAN
- DAIRY-FREE
- NUT-FREE
- GLUTEN-FREE

BREAKFAST
Strawberry, Grapefruit, and Ginger Smoothie

page 110

• • • •

Start your morning with this antioxidant-packed smoothie.

LUNCH
Beet, Avocado, and Arugula Salad with Sunflower Seeds

page 150

• • • •

Refuel at midday with a fiber-filled meal to keep you satisfied through the afternoon.

DINNER
Carrot, Spinach, and Green Bean Soup with Dill

page 183

• • • •

Soothe the stomach with this purifying dish, which also delivers a second serving of nutrition-packed leafy greens.

21-day action plan

Increased energy, sound sleep, weight loss, greater self-knowledge: That's what you can expect to gain with this three-week plan, which promotes a diet heavy on whole foods. Week one is about cleaning the slate, while weeks two and three are about focusing on awareness and forming healthy habits.

WEEK 1: pare down and purify

You'll start off by detoxing with a spare diet meant to give your digestive system the rest it needs. By midweek, you'll likely notice some unpleasant symptoms—fatigue, aches and pains, headache, bloat—all signs that your body is purging toxins. This is normal (and temporary), so don't lose heart.

ONE-WEEK OPTION
While you'll get the most benefits if you complete the full three weeks, you can opt for a 7-Day Detox instead. Simply follow the guidelines for Week 1, and then ease back into your regular diet.

WHAT'S ON THE MENU
Legumes, fruits and vegetables, nuts and seeds, and oils and seasonings are the only ingredients allowed in the first week. Breakfasts are juices and smoothies. Lunches and dinners include lots of liver-boosting vegetables and legumes.

BASE DIET
- Legumes
- Fruits and vegetables
- Nuts and seeds
- Oils and seasonings

MEDITATION OF THE WEEK
Think about your relationship with food. Separating physical nourishment from emotional comfort helps you make better choices, eating-wise.

GET MOVING
Since you're scaling back the protein, skip strength training and anything that's strenuous or done in a heated room, like Bikram yoga. Focus on stimulating your elimination organs, including the liver and kidneys, with gentle stretches and mellow cardio, such as walking. Stretch for 10 minutes five mornings this week, and complete 30 minutes of gentle to moderate cardio on three of the days.

ICONS
- VEGAN
- DAIRY-FREE
- NUT-FREE
- GLUTEN-FREE

DAY	BREAKFAST	LUNCH	DINNER
1	Green Machine Smoothie, *page 111* • • • •	Brussels Sprout Salad with Avocado and Pumpkin Seeds, *page 154* • • • •	Pureed Cauliflower Soup, *page 152* • • •
2	Cucumber-Pear Juice, *page 116* • • • •	Red Lentil Soup with Turnip and Parsley, *page 266* • • • •	Cauliflower "Rice" Stir-Fry with Pumpkin Seeds, *page 163* • • • •
3	Coconut-Cherry Smoothie, *page 112* • • • •	Beet, Avocado, and Arugula Salad with Sunflower Seeds, *page 150* • • • •	Pureed Cauliflower Soup, *page 152* • • •
4	Pineapple-Spinach Juice, *page 117* • • • •	Cauliflower "Rice" Stir-Fry with Pumpkin Seeds, *page 163* • • • •	Roasted Portobellos with Kale and Red Onion, *page 159* • • •
5	Green Machine Smoothie, *page 111* • • • •	Beet, Avocado, and Arugula Salad with Sunflower Seeds, *page 150* • • • •	Red Lentil Soup with Turnip and Parsley, *page 266* • • • •
6	Green Goodness Juice, *page 112* • • • •	Brussels Sprout Salad with Avocado and Pumpkin Seeds, *page 154* • • • •	Roasted Portobellos with Kale and Red Onion, *page 159* • • •
7	Coconut-Cherry Smoothie, *page 112* • • • •	Beet, Avocado, and Arugula Salad with Sunflower Seeds, *page 150* • • • •	Cauliflower "Rice" Stir-Fry with Pumpkin Seeds, *page 163* • • • •

WEEK 2: focus on awareness

Now that you've detoxed for a whole week, you're ready to expand your diet. As you reintroduce some clean animal proteins and gluten-free grains, notice how you feel. "Removing food for just a week is often long enough to observe if this food is a match for you or if it causes an adverse reaction," says nutritionist Kathie Madonna Swift. If the excitement you felt in week one starts to fade, revisit your goals and recommit.

HYDRATION IS KEY

It's important to get enough fluids during the day (see "Remember to Stay Hydrated," page 28), but even more so when cleansing. Fluids flush toxins and keep hunger at bay. Start the morning with hot water and a squeeze of lemon, and drink plenty of water all day.

WHAT'S ON THE MENU

This week you'll find gluten-free whole grains like quinoa and brown rice and heartier proteins like wild Alaskan salmon and sardines. Coming off last week's light fare, you'll begin to build back your strength and feel satisfied. Cook the grains and make the big-batch breakfast soup ahead. You'll save yourself time during the week.

ADD BACK
• Fish (except shellfish)
• Gluten-free grains

MEDITATION OF THE WEEK

Think before you eat. Take five deep, slow breaths before every meal, and give each bite your full attention.

GET MOVING

The carbs and seafood should lift your energy, so it's time to step up the intensity of your exercise—and step outside. Being in nature makes working out a pleasure. Aim to stretch for 10 minutes four mornings this week and complete 30 minutes of cardio at a low to moderate intensity three days this week (think walking, hiking, or dancing). But if the goals this week seem too rigorous, simply continue with the moves from last week.

ICONS
● VEGAN
● DAIRY-FREE
● NUT-FREE
● GLUTEN-FREE

DAY	BREAKFAST	LUNCH	DINNER
8	Cardamom Quinoa Porridge with Pear, *page 104* ● ● ●	Watercress, Sardine, and Orange Salad, *page 280* ● ● ●	Shiitake Mushrooms and Brown Rice in Parchment, *page 249* ● ● ● ●
9	Millet with Pineapple, Coconut, and Flaxseed, *page 95* ● ● ●	Quinoa Salad with Zucchini, Mint, and Pistachios, *page 134* ● ● ●	Grilled Salmon and Bok Choy with Orange-Avocado Salsa, *page 276* ● ● ●
10	Breakfast Vegetable-Miso Soup with Chickpeas, *page 102* ● ● ● ●	Roasted Vegetables with Quinoa, *page 120* ● ● ● ●	Baked Sweet Potato with Greens, *page 132* ● ● ● ●
11	Cardamom Quinoa Porridge with Pear, *page 104* ● ● ●	Shiitake Mushrooms and Brown Rice in Parchment, *page 249* ● ● ● ●	Grilled Salmon and Bok Choy with Orange-Avocado Salsa, *page 276* ● ● ●
12	Breakfast Vegetable-Miso Soup with Chickpeas, *page 102* ● ● ● ●	Watercress, Sardine, and Orange Salad, *page 280* ● ● ●	Roasted Vegetables with Quinoa, *page 120* ● ● ● ●
13	Millet with Pineapple, Coconut, and Flaxseed, *page 95* ● ● ●	Baked Sweet Potato with Greens, *page 132* ● ● ● ●	Quinoa Salad with Zucchini, Mint, and Pistachios, *page 134* ● ● ●
14	Cardamom Quinoa Porridge with Pear, *page 104* ● ● ●	Shiitake Mushrooms and Brown Rice in Parchment, *page 249* ● ● ● ●	Roasted Vegetables with Quinoa, *page 120* ● ● ● ●

WEEK 3: form healthy habits

With two full weeks behind you, and any negative detox symptoms also relegated to the past, clean eating will start to feel less like a burden and more like a lifestyle. You should feel lighter (you've likely dropped a few pounds) and be conscious of the impacts—improved digestion, more energy, better sleep—of a healthy diet. Keep it up. Focus not just on what you're restricting, but on what you're bringing to your diet: more fruits and vegetables and whole grains. You've raised the bar on health, and, after this week, the goal will be to keep it there.

BACK IN ACTION

The time has come to cement your newfound healthy eating habits into a cooking regimen that will really last. Focus on how to get healthy carbohydrates, proteins, and fats into every meal. Increase your plant-to-animal ratio. And, if you're a meat eater, opt for grass-fed meats, but eat them sparingly.

WHAT'S ON THE MENU

Two foods often related to sensitivities reenter the mix this week: soy (tofu, edamame) and eggs, which are commonly associated with digestive symptoms. Pay close attention to how you feel: This is information-gathering time.

ADD BACK

- Organic (non-GMO) soy
- Eggs

MEDITATION OF THE WEEK

As you inhale, focus on a soothing phrase, such as "I'm happy and healthy." You can say it aloud or in your mind. When exhaling, silently repeat the mantra. The specific phrase isn't that important; the mantra's purpose is to give your mind something simple to focus on.

GET MOVING

Now that you're enjoying a nourishing and sustainable diet, lock in an exercise schedule that you can keep up all year. Aim to: Stretch for 10 minutes five mornings this week; complete one 60-minute and two 30-minute cardio sessions three days; and strength-train (aim for 60 minutes total, spread over a few sessions) three to four days.

ICONS

- VEGAN
- DAIRY-FREE
- NUT-FREE
- GLUTEN-FREE

DAY	BREAKFAST	LUNCH	DINNER
15	Frittata with Spring Vegetables, *page 79* • • •	Fennel, Sunchoke, and Green Apple Salad, *page 122* • •	Roasted Squash with Grains, Grapes, and Sage, *page 147* • • •
16	Black Quinoa with Avocado, Almonds, and Honey, *page 96* • •	Poached Egg with Rice and Edamame, *page 230* • • •	Trout, Tomatoes, and Basil in Parchment, *page 270* • • •
17	Banana-Apple Buckwheat Muffins, *page 90* • •	Grapefruit, Salmon, and Avocado Salad, *page 265* • • •	Spinach, Tofu, and Brown Rice Bowl, *page 237* • • • •
18	Black Quinoa with Avocado, Almonds, and Honey, *page 96* • •	Fennel, Sunchoke, and Green Apple Salad, *page 122* • •	Poached Egg with Rice and Edamame, *page 230* • • •
19	Banana-Apple Buckwheat Muffins, *page 90* • •	Roasted Squash with Grains, Grapes, and Sage, *page 147* • • •	Trout, Tomatoes, and Basil in Parchment, *page 270* • • •
20	Frittata with Spring Vegetables, *page 79* • • •	Fennel, Sunchoke, and Green Apple Salad, *page 122* • •	Spinach, Tofu, and Brown Rice Bowl, *page 237* • • • •
21	Black Quinoa with Avocado, Almonds, and Honey, *page 96* • •	Grapefruit, Salmon, and Avocado Salad, *page 265* • • •	Poached Egg with Rice and Edamame, *page 230* • • •

recipes

replenish

---

get off to a good start

You've heard it a thousand times—skipping breakfast is a bad idea—and it's true. Breaking the fast is essential to regulating metabolism and blood sugar, and it provides the brainpower you need to function at your very best, all day.

NUT-FREE

PER SERVING 447 CALORIES, 19 G FAT (3 G
SATURATED FAT), 61 MG CHOLESTEROL, 57 G
CARBOHYDRATES, 17 G PROTEIN, 7 G FIBER

whole-wheat waffles with sliced strawberries and yogurt

It's hard to believe these crisp, light waffles are made with only whole-wheat flour (and toasted wheat germ); make sure to use a regular variety of whole-wheat flour—not stone ground, which would produce a heavier texture. You can use this recipe to make fluffy pancakes, too. *Serves 4*

1½ cups whole-wheat flour (not stone ground)

2 tablespoons toasted wheat germ

2 tablespoons cane sugar

1½ teaspoons baking powder

½ teaspoon coarse salt

1½ cups milk

¼ cup canola oil, plus more for waffle iron

1 large egg

1 teaspoon pure vanilla extract

1 cup plain Greek yogurt

1 pint strawberries, hulled and sliced

Pure maple syrup, for serving

Preheat a waffle iron (preferably Belgian-style). Whisk together flour, wheat germ, sugar, baking powder, and salt. In another bowl, whisk together milk, oil, egg, and vanilla. Stir milk mixture into flour mixture until just combined.

Brush oil over waffle iron. Ladle ½ cup batter onto each square of the grid (or according to manufacturer's instructions), and cook until golden brown. Top with yogurt, strawberries, and syrup and serve immediately.

coconut breakfast pudding with sautéed nectarines

Pudding for breakfast? Sure, when it's made from old-fashioned rolled oats and unsweetened fiber-rich coconut, which are soaked together overnight for a rich, creamy consistency. Coconut oil is a good source of antioxidants; look for organic, unrefined, expeller-pressed coconut oil at health-food stores and some supermarkets. *Serves 2*

⅔ cup old-fashioned rolled oats (not quick-cooking)

⅓ cup unsweetened shredded coconut

1½ cups water

1 cup unsweetened almond milk (see recipe, page 315)

⅛ teaspoon ground cinnamon
Pinch of coarse salt

2 teaspoons organic unrefined coconut oil

2 nectarines, pitted and sliced

1 tablespoon pure maple syrup, plus more for serving (optional)

¼ cup unsweetened large coconut flakes, toasted (see page 314)

Combine oats and shredded coconut with the water in a bowl. Cover and refrigerate overnight.

Transfer oat mixture to a medium saucepan. Add milk, cinnamon, and salt; bring to a boil. Reduce heat to low, and simmer, covered, until creamy, about 12 minutes. Remove from heat, stir to combine, and cover to keep warm.

Heat oil in a medium skillet over medium-high. Add nectarines and sauté until golden, stirring frequently, 1 to 2 minutes. Stir in maple syrup.

Divide oats between 2 bowls, and top with nectarines and coconut flakes. Serve drizzled with additional syrup, if desired.

VEGAN DAIRY-FREE

PER SERVING 453 CALORIES, 25 G FAT (19 G
SATURATED FAT), 0 MG CHOLESTEROL, 50 G
CARBOHYDRATES, 8 G PROTEIN, 9 G FIBER

DAIRY-FREE **NUT-FREE** GLUTEN-FREE

PER SERVING 225 CALORIES, 154 G FAT (37 G
SATURATED FAT), 423 MG CHOLESTEROL, 5 G
CARBOHYDRATES, 14 G PROTEIN, 1 G FIBER

frittata with spring vegetables

An Italian frittata is a great make-ahead—and healthful—brunch option. This one is filled with zucchini, asparagus, and sliced jalapeño. Serve leftover frittata (it's good cold, at room temperature, or rewarmed in the oven) with some leafy greens for lunch or a light dinner. *Serves 4*

2 tablespoons extra-virgin olive oil

½ small red onion, thinly sliced

1 jalapeño chile, thinly sliced (ribs and seeds removed for less heat, if desired)

1 zucchini, thinly sliced

¼ bunch asparagus (4 ounces), ends trimmed, tips cut into 2-inch pieces and stalks cut into ¼-inch pieces

Coarse salt

8 large eggs

Heat broiler. In an ovenproof skillet, heat oil over medium. Add onion and jalapeño; cook, stirring, until tender, about 5 minutes. Add zucchini and asparagus; cook until tender, stirring, about 7 minutes more. Season with salt.

Whisk eggs in a bowl; season with salt. Pour into skillet with vegetables; cook, undisturbed, until sides just begin to set, 2 to 3 minutes.

Transfer skillet to oven; broil until frittata is just set in the middle and lightly golden and puffed on top, 2 to 3 minutes. Serve warm or at room temperature.

steamed salmon
with avocado

This heart-healthy morning meal is an excellent way to fill up on omega-3s and lean protein. Steam the salmon the night before and breakfast is ready in a snap. *Serves 1*

1 lemon, ½ sliced into thin rounds, ½ cut into wedges for serving

1 skinless wild salmon fillet (about 4 ounces)

Flaky sea salt (such as Maldon) and freshly ground pepper

½ ripe but firm avocado, peeled and sliced

Rustic whole-grain bread, toasted, for serving (optional)

Arrange lemon rounds on bottom of a steamer basket or colander. Season salmon with sea salt and pepper. Place salmon on top of lemons.

Bring about 1 inch water to a simmer in a large saucepan. Place steamer basket in pan, cover, and steam until fish is cooked through, about 7 minutes.

Arrange avocado and salmon on plates. Sprinkle salmon with sea salt and pepper. Serve with lemon wedges and toast, if desired.

DAIRY-FREE NUT-FREE

PER SERVING 317 CALORIES, 21 G FAT (3 G
SATURATED FAT), 62 MG CHOLESTEROL, 12 G
CARBOHYDRATES, 24 G PROTEIN, 6 G FIBER

GLUTEN-FREE

PER SERVING 173 CALORIES, 6 G FAT (2 G
SATURATED FAT), 8 MG CHOLESTEROL, 22 G
CARBOHYDRATES, 12 G PROTEIN, 2 G FIBER

honey-caramelized figs with yogurt

There's nothing quite like the taste of fresh figs—luscious, sweet, and slightly crunchy with tiny seeds. They're even better when caramelized, which takes mere minutes on the stove. Serve them warm over your morning yogurt (as done here) or steel-cut oatmeal, or topped with fresh ricotta for a snack or dessert. *Serves 4*

1 tablespoon honey, plus more for serving (optional)

8 ounces fresh figs, halved

2 cups plain Greek yogurt

Pinch of ground cinnamon

¼ cup chopped shelled pistachios

Heat honey in a skillet over medium. Add figs, cut sides down, and cook until caramelized, about 5 minutes. Let cool slightly.

Serve over yogurt, topped with cinnamon and pistachios. Drizzle with additional honey, if desired.

crostini with fresh ricotta, cherries, and lemon zest

Here's a novel and tasty topping for toast, instead of jam and butter: fresh ricotta and chopped cherries—among the best sources of antioxidants. The cherries are macerated with a bit of brown sugar for added sweetness and to extract juices, but you could omit this step. *Serves 4*

6 ounces sweet cherries, pitted and chopped (1¼ cups)

1 tablespoon packed light-brown sugar

4 slices rustic bread

2 tablespoons extra-virgin olive oil

½ cup fresh ricotta

Grated zest of 1 lemon, plus more for garnish (peeled in long strips)

Preheat oven to 375°F. Combine cherries and brown sugar in a bowl; let macerate 10 minutes.

Meanwhile, brush bread with olive oil, and toast until golden, 5 to 7 minutes. Mix together ricotta and lemon zest in a bowl.

Dividing evenly, spread ricotta on bread and top with cherries. Garnish with zest and serve immediately.

NUT-FREE

PER SERVING 261 CALORIES, 12 G FAT (4 G
SATURATED FAT), 16 MG CHOLESTEROL, 31 G
CARBOHYDRATES, 8 G PROTEIN, 3 G FIBER

tofu scramble
with cotija cheese
and tortillas

You can still enjoy your favorite Mexican-style breakfasts on a clean diet. Just tweak them slightly to include healthier ingredients. In this version, tofu and black beans are sautéed with garlic, chile, and spices, then served over toasted corn tortillas. Using a strong-flavored cheese like cotija means you need only a small amount. *Serves 4*

1 tablespoon extra-virgin olive oil

1 garlic clove, minced

1 serrano chile, minced (ribs and seeds removed, if desired)

2 scallions, whites and greens separated, thinly sliced

½ teaspoon ground cumin

½ teaspoon dried oregano

½ teaspoon ground turmeric

14 ounces soft tofu, drained and crumbled into large pieces

1 cup cooked black beans, drained and rinsed (see page 54)

Coarse salt

8 corn tortillas (6-inch size)

1 avocado, halved, pitted, peeled, and sliced

½ cup cotija cheese, crumbled (2 ounces)

Heat oil in a skillet over medium. Add garlic, serrano, and scallion whites; cook until tender, stirring frequently, about 2 minutes. Add cumin, oregano, and turmeric; cook, stirring, 1 minute. Stir in tofu and beans; cook, stirring, until heated through, about 4 minutes. Season with salt, and sprinkle with scallion greens. Remove from heat.

Meanwhile, toast tortillas over a gas burner, turning with tongs, until lightly charred, about 1 minute (or char under the broiler).

Serve tortillas filled with tofu scramble, avocado, and cotija, dividing evenly.

NUT-FREE GLUTEN-FREE

PER SERVING 357 CALORIES, 16 G FAT (3 G
SATURATED FAT), 5 MG CHOLESTEROL, 42 G
CARBOHYDRATES, 15 G PROTEIN, 11 G FIBER

PER SERVING 244 CALORIES, 9 G FAT (1 G
SATURATED FAT), 4 MG CHOLESTEROL, 37 G
CARBOHYDRATES, 7 G PROTEIN, 4 G FIBER

fruit and almond alpine muesli

This nourishing, no-cook breakfast cereal features a neat trick from the Swiss: The oats are mixed with yogurt and milk, then refrigerated for several hours, so the grains soak up the liquid and soften. It is also packed with nuts and fruit—some chopped and mixed in, the rest served on top. Use a mix of whatever fruit is in season. *Serves 8*

⅔ cup plain yogurt (not Greek)

⅔ cup milk

1 teaspoon pure vanilla extract

Pinch of coarse salt

1½ cups old-fashioned rolled oats (not quick-cooking)

¼ cup plus 1 tablespoon honey

⅔ cup fresh orange juice (from 2 oranges)

2 Granny Smith apples, peeled

1 cup chopped almonds

2 cups finely chopped seasonal fruits (such as plums, strawberries, and peaches)

Seasonal fruits (such as sliced oranges, strawberries and plums, and whole or sliced raspberries and blackberries), for serving

Whisk together yogurt, milk, vanilla, and salt in a bowl until smooth. Stir in oats. Cover and refrigerate at least 3 hours and up to overnight.

Stir together ¼ cup honey and the orange juice in a bowl. Grate apples on the large holes of a box grater. Stir apples and almonds into juice mixture. Stir apple mixture into soaked oats until well combined. Gently mix in chopped fruit. Refrigerate 30 minutes.

To serve, top muesli with more fruit, and drizzle with remaining tablespoon honey.

banana-apple buckwheat muffins

Many gluten-free muffins call for a combination of flours, but these simplify the process by using just one type—protein-rich buckwheat flour. Honey adds sweetness; mashed banana and diced apple keep them moist. Store muffins in the freezer, wrapped tightly, up to three months. *Makes 12*

½ cup buckwheat flour

2 teaspoons baking powder

1 teaspoon ground cinnamon

¼ teaspoon coarse salt

4 large eggs

1 ripe banana, mashed

½ cup honey

1½ cups finely chopped (peeled and cored) sweet apple, such as Honeycrisp (1 apple)

½ cup chopped walnuts

Preheat oven to 350°F. Line a standard muffin tin with paper liners.

Whisk together flour, baking powder, cinnamon, and salt. In another bowl, whisk together eggs, banana, and honey. Mix banana mixture into flour mixture, then fold in apple and walnuts (batter will be thin).

Divide batter among lined cups, filling to top. Bake until a toothpick inserted in center comes out clean, about 30 minutes. Transfer muffins to a wire rack to cool. Store in an airtight container at room temperature up to 2 days.

DAIRY-FREE GLUTEN-FREE

PER SERVING (1 MUFFIN) 196 CALORIES, 8 G FAT
(1 G SATURATED FAT), 106 MG CHOLESTEROL, 30 G
CARBOHYDRATES, 6 G PROTEIN, 2 G FIBER

sardines and cream cheese on rye

Rye toast topped with sardines provides a similar savory kick as bagels and lox, in a much more nutritious package. The little cold-water fish are loaded with omega-3s, protein, and calcium, while whole-grain rye bread has more fiber than wheat. Neufchâtel is naturally lower in fat than regular cream cheese, without any of the fillers of reduced-fat versions. *Serves 4*

¼ cup Neufchâtel or cream cheese (2 ounces)

4 slices rye bread, toasted

1 tin (4.4 ounces) olive-oil-packed sardines, drained

¼ small red onion, thinly sliced

2 tablespoons chopped fresh dill

Coarse salt and freshly ground pepper

Spread 1 tablespoon Neufchâtel on each bread slice. Top with sardines, red onion, and dill, dividing evenly. Season with salt and pepper, and serve.

NUT-FREE

PER SERVING 190 CALORIES, 8 G FAT (3 G
SATURATED FAT), 55 MG CHOLESTEROL, 17 G
CARBOHYDRATES, 12 G PROTEIN, 2 G FIBER

millet with pineapple, coconut, and flaxseed

When it comes to breakfast porridges, there's a world of different grains to explore. Millet, for one, is both gluten-free and an excellent source of magnesium, important for heart health. Here, it serves as the whole-grain base for a tropical mix of pineapple and toasted coconut. (See pages 96 and 97 for the other recipes shown opposite.) *Serves 4*

6 cups water

Pinch of coarse salt

1 cup millet

½ cup unsweetened almond milk (see recipe, page 315) or coconut milk

½ cup chopped fresh pineapple

¼ cup large-flake unsweetened coconut, toasted (see page 314)

1 tablespoon plus 1 teaspoon whole flaxseed

¼ cup pure maple syrup

Bring the water and salt to a boil in a medium saucepan. Whisk in millet. Return to a boil. Reduce heat to low, and simmer, covered, until water has been absorbed and millet is tender but still chewy, 30 to 35 minutes. Remove from heat; let stand 5 minutes, then fluff with a fork. Serve topped with milk, pineapple, coconut, flaxseed, and maple syrup.

VEGAN DAIRY-FREE GLUTEN-FREE

PER SERVING 316 CALORIES, 7 G FAT (4 G SATURATED FAT), 0 MG CHOLESTEROL, 56 G CARBOHYDRATES, 7 G PROTEIN, 6 G FIBER

black quinoa with avocado, almonds, and honey

Black quinoa (like red quinoa) has a firmer, crunchier texture and a more pronounced flavor than the white variety, but you can use any kind of quinoa in this recipe. Topped with avocado, almonds, and honey, this is a truly habit-forming breakfast. *Serves 6*

2 cups water

Pinch of coarse salt

1 cup black (or red) quinoa, rinsed and drained

1½ cups unsweetened almond milk (see recipe, page 315)

1 avocado, halved, pitted, peeled, and sliced

¼ cup plus 2 tablespoons sliced almonds, toasted (see page 314)

¼ cup plus 2 tablespoons honey

Bring the water and salt to a boil in a medium saucepan. Whisk in quinoa. Return to a boil. Reduce heat to low, and simmer, covered, until water has been absorbed and quinoa is tender but still chewy, about 15 minutes. Remove from heat; let stand 5 minutes, then fluff with a fork. Serve topped with milk, avocado, almonds, and honey, dividing evenly.

DAIRY-FREE GLUTEN-FREE

PER SERVING 269 CALORIES, 16 G FAT (1 G SATURATED FAT), 0 MG CHOLESTEROL, 43 G CARBOHYDRATES, 6 G PROTEIN, 5 G FIBER

barley with apricots, hazelnuts, chocolate, and honey

Having a little dark chocolate at breakfast will add a dose of antioxidants, not to mention a touch of indulgence, to your morning. Be sure to use chocolate with at least 70 percent cacao. *Serves 4*

2½ cups water

    Pinch of coarse salt

 1 cup pearl barley

 1 cup buttermilk

¼ cup chopped dried apricots

¼ cup blanched and chopped hazelnuts (see page 314)

¼ cup chopped dark chocolate (at least 70 percent cacao)

¼ cup honey

Bring the water and salt to a boil in a medium saucepan. Whisk in barley. Return to a boil. Reduce heat to low, and simmer, covered, until water has been absorbed and barley is tender but still chewy, about 1 hour. Remove from heat; let stand 5 minutes, then fluff with a fork. Serve topped with buttermilk, apricots, hazelnuts, chocolate, and honey.

PER SERVING 387 CALORIES, 9 G FAT (2 G SATURATED FAT), 2 MG CHOLESTEROL, 73 G CARBOHYDRATES, 9 G PROTEIN, 10 G FIBER

poached eggs
with roasted tomatoes

Roasting coaxes flavor from even out-of-season tomatoes; you can also try them tossed with pasta or added to salads. Here, they make the perfect accompaniment to poached eggs in open-faced breakfast sandwiches. *Serves 2*

1 pint cherry tomatoes (10 ounces)

1 tablespoon extra-virgin olive oil

Coarse salt and freshly ground pepper

1 tablespoon fresh thyme leaves, plus more for garnish

2 large eggs

1 whole-wheat English muffin, split and toasted

Preheat oven to 425°F. Place tomatoes in a baking dish. Drizzle with oil, and season with salt and pepper. Add thyme and toss to combine. Spread in a single layer, and roast until tomatoes begin to burst, about 20 minutes. Transfer tomatoes and any juices to a bowl, and let cool slightly.

Bring 3 inches of water to a simmer in a skillet. Crack one egg at a time into a teacup or small bowl, and gently slide into water. Cook until whites are just set and yolks are still loose, 3 to 4 minutes. Using a slotted spoon, transfer each egg to an English muffin half. Season with salt and pepper.

Top with roasted tomatoes, dividing evenly. Garnish with thyme. Serve immediately.

DAIRY-FREE NUT-FREE

PER SERVING 230 CALORIES, 13 G FAT (3 G
SATURATED FAT), 212 MG CHOLESTEROL, 20 G
CARBOHYDRATES, 10 G PROTEIN, 4 G FIBER

PER SERVING 193 CALORIES, 7 G FAT (0 G
SATURATED FAT), 0 MG CHOLESTEROL 29 G
CARBOHYDRATES, 6 G PROTEIN, 4 G FIBER

mixed-grain
and almond granola

Bake a batch of this whole-grain cereal at the beginning of the week for instant breakfasts (and portable snacking). Rolled barley and spelt flakes, such as those by Bob's Red Mill, are available at health food stores and many supermarkets, as well as online. You can also make this recipe using only rolled oats (3 cups total). Here, the granola makes a crunchy topping for yogurt, along with blueberries (or any fresh fruit). *Serves 10*

1 cup rolled barley flakes

1 cup rolled spelt flakes

1 cup old-fashioned rolled oats (not quick-cooking)

1 cup sliced almonds

⅓ cup pure maple syrup

2 tablespoons light-brown sugar

⅓ cup extra-virgin olive oil

1 teaspoon pure vanilla extract

½ teaspoon coarse salt

Preheat oven to 325°F. Toss to combine all ingredients in a bowl, then spread in a single layer on a rimmed baking sheet. Bake, stirring halfway through, until golden brown, about 30 minutes. Let cool completely. Store granola in an airtight container at room temperature up to 3 weeks.

breakfast
vegetable-miso soup
with chickpeas

Rethink your idea of breakfast to include savory dishes like this nourishing soup. You'll get a head start on meeting your daily quotient of vegetables—plus legumes to boot. White miso adds a bit of extra protein as well as flavor. *Serves 4*

2 tablespoons extra-virgin olive oil

½ yellow onion, chopped

2 celery stalks, diced

2 carrots, diced

2 garlic cloves, minced

1 cup chopped broccoli florets

1 cup cooked chickpeas, drained and rinsed (see page 54)

4 cups water

2 tablespoons shiro (white) miso

Coarse salt

Heat oil in a medium saucepan over medium. Add onion, celery, carrots, and garlic; cook until tender, stirring occasionally, 6 to 8 minutes. Stir in broccoli and chickpeas; cook, stirring, 2 minutes.

Add the water, and bring to a boil. Reduce heat to low, and simmer, covered, until vegetables are tender, about 10 minutes. Remove from heat. Remove 2 tablespoons liquid; dissolve miso in liquid, then stir into soup. Season with salt and serve immediately.

VEGAN DAIRY-FREE **NUT-FREE** GLUTEN-FREE

PER SERVING 180 CALORIES, 8 G FAT (1 G
SATURATED FAT), 0 MG CHOLESTEROL, 23 G
CARBOHYDRATES, 6 G PROTEIN, 6 G FIBER

cardamom quinoa porridge
with pear

Cardamom, long used for its medicinal properties in Eastern cultures, has been shown to improve energy—making it an invigorating addition to your morning meal. For best results, buy whole cardamom pods and grind them as needed. *Serves 2*

½ cup quinoa, rinsed and drained

1¾ cups unsweetened almond milk (see recipe, page 315)

½ cup water

½ teaspoon pure vanilla extract

¼ teaspoon ground cardamom
    Pinch of coarse salt

1 pear, cored and chopped

¼ cup sliced almonds, toasted (see page 314)

In a medium saucepan, bring quinoa, ¾ cup milk, the water, vanilla, cardamom, and salt to a boil. Reduce heat to low, and simmer, covered, until liquid has been absorbed and quinoa is tender but still chewy, about 15 minutes. Remove from heat; let stand 5 minutes, then fluff with a fork. Serve topped with remaining cup milk, the pear, and almonds.

VEGAN DAIRY-FREE GLUTEN-FREE

PER SERVING 334 CALORIES, 11 G FAT (1 G
SATURATED FAT), 0 MG CHOLESTEROL, 52 G
CARBOHYDRATES, 9 G PROTEIN, 8 G FIBER

mushroom and microgreen omelet

Unlike sprouts, which are germinated in water for just forty-eight hours, microgreens are grown in soil and sunlight for at least seven days. The nutrients in these vitamin-and-mineral-packed seedlings are more concentrated than in a full-grown plant. Look for them at farmers' markets and natural-food stores. Pea shoots or baby lettuces (tatsoi or spinach) make fine substitutes. *Serves 1*

1 tablespoon olive oil

½ cup thinly sliced button mushrooms

Coarse salt and freshly ground pepper

¾ cup microgreens

3 large eggs

Heat 1½ teaspoons oil in a small nonstick skillet over medium-high. Add mushrooms and cook, undisturbed, until they begin to release their liquid, about 2 minutes; season with salt and pepper. Cook until golden brown, stirring occasionally, about 2 minutes more. Transfer mushrooms to a bowl, and stir in microgreens.

Whisk eggs in another bowl; season with salt and pepper. Wipe skillet clean with paper towels. Heat remaining 1½ teaspoons oil over medium. Pour eggs into skillet; cook, undisturbed, until edges are set slightly. With a heatproof flexible spatula, push eggs from edge toward center, tilting pan to let uncooked eggs run underneath, until omelet is just set, 1 to 2 minutes. Place mushroom filling on one side of omelet. Using spatula, gently fold other side of omelet over filling. Serve immediately.

DAIRY-FREE **NUT-FREE** GLUTEN-FREE

PER SERVING 355 CALORIES, 29 G FAT (7 G
SATURATED FAT), 635 MG CHOLESTEROL, 4 G
CARBOHYDRATES, 21 G PROTEIN, 1 G FIBER

reboot

---

drink to your health

Juices and smoothies offer a lot of bang for the buck, nutrient-wise. This collection contains several master formulas to help you feel your best, whether your aim is to detoxify, boost your antioxidants, hydrate, get energized—or all of the above.

detoxifying You don't have to be on a cleanse to benefit from these tonics; try one whenever you're feeling sluggish (or to prevent feeling that way).

combine in a juicer:

2 cored and chopped tart apples

1 chopped English cucumber

½ chopped lemon

Pinch of cayenne pepper

serves 2

↓

apple, cucumber, and lemon juice

combine in a blender:

2 cups hulled strawberries

1 peeled, seeded, and chopped grapefruit

1 cored and chopped sweet apple

1 cup water

1-inch piece fresh ginger, peeled and chopped

serves 3

↓

strawberry, grapefruit, and ginger smoothie

combine in a juicer:

1 stemmed and chopped bunch kale

1 chopped fennel bulb

1 cored and chopped Granny Smith apple

¼ chopped honeydew

1 celery stalk

1-inch piece fresh ginger, peeled and chopped

serves 2

↓

ultra-green juice

combine in a juicer:

5 chopped carrots

1 chopped small beet

1 cored and chopped
sweet apple

¼ cup mint leaves

serves 1

↓

beet,
apple, and
mint juice

combine in a juicer:

2 peeled, seeded, and
chopped grapefruits

5 chopped carrots

1-inch piece fresh
ginger, peeled and
chopped

serves 1

↓

grapefruit,
carrot, and
ginger juice

combine in a blender:

6 chopped romaine
leaves

4 stemmed and chopped
kale leaves

1½ cups water

½ cup chopped
pineapple

½ cup parsley leaves

½ cup chopped mango

1-inch piece fresh
ginger, peeled and
chopped

serves 2

↓

green
machine
smoothie

anti-inflammatory Preventive medicine in a glass: A rainbow of fruits and vegetables, plus green tea and potent spices, will keep you feeling your best.

combine in a blender:

1 cup chopped spinach

1 stemmed and chopped large kale leaf

1 cored and chopped apple

½ cup water or coconut water

¼ cup fresh blueberries

½ chopped lemon

½-inch piece fresh ginger, peeled and chopped

serves 2

↓

combine in a blender:

1½ cups chopped papaya

1 cup ice

2 tablespoons honey

1 teaspoon chia seeds, soaked in 1 cup cold water 10 minutes

¼ teaspoon turmeric

1 teaspoon grated peeled fresh ginger

Pinch of cayenne pepper

serves 2

↓

combine in a blender:

2 cups frozen pitted cherries

1 cup coconut water

1 tablespoon lime juice

serves 2

↓

coconut-cherry
smoothie

spiced papaya
smoothie

green goodness
juice

PER SERVING 115 CALORIES
● ● ● ●

PER SERVING 57 CALORIES
● ● ●

PER SERVING 73 CALORIES
● ● ● ●

combine in a blender:

1½ cups frozen
blackberries

1 cup orange juice

1 pitted and chopped
black plum

serves 2

↓

combine in a juicer:

2 cups baby spinach

2 cored and chopped
sweet apples

1 chopped cucumber

½ chopped lemon

serves 1

↓

combine in a blender:

1½ cups green tea,
frozen in an
ice-cube tray

½ cup chilled green tea

½ cup fresh blueberries

1 tablespoon honey

serves 2

↓

blackberry-plum
smoothie

spinach-apple
juice

blueberry—green tea
smoothie

PER SERVING 143 CALORIES
● ● ● ●

PER SERVING 219 CALORIES
● ● ● ●

PER SERVING 53 CALORIES
● ● ●

energizing Make one of these protein-packed smoothies whenever you need a boost. They're loaded with nut and seed butters, yogurt, tofu, and more.

combine in a blender:

1 cup plain yogurt

1 cup apple cider or juice

1 cup ice

3 tablespoons almond butter

4 pitted dates

serves 2

↓

almond-date
smoothie

combine in a blender:

1 cup ice

½ peeled avocado

½ cup coconut water

¼ cup plain yogurt

¼ teaspoon pure vanilla extract

1 tablespoon honey

serves 2

↓

avocado-yogurt
smoothie

combine in a blender:

¾ cup fresh blueberries

½ cup plain yogurt

½ cup ice

2 tablespoons orange juice

2 tablespoons unsweetened almond milk

1 tablespoon honey

serves 1

↓

blueberry-yogurt
smoothie

combine in a blender:

1 cup stemmed and
chopped kale leaves,
steamed and cooled

1 cup coconut water

1 peeled, cored, and
chopped sweet apple

1 tablespoon sunflower-
seed butter

1 tablespoon honey

serves 2

↓

sweet **kale-
sunflower**
smoothie

PER SERVING 149 CALORIES
● ● ●

---

combine in a blender:

2½ peeled, cored, and
chopped pears

1¾ cups milk

1 cup buttermilk

⅔ cup oats

⅓ cup ice cubes

2½ tablespoons
maple syrup

2 tablespoons
almond butter

1¼ teaspoons grated
peeled fresh ginger

⅛ teaspoon cinnamon

Pinch of coarse salt

serves 4

↓

pear, oat,
and **ginger**
smoothie

PER SERVING 266 CALORIES
●

---

combine in a blender:

2 cups frozen mixed
berries

½ cup silken tofu

½ cup orange juice

1 peeled banana

serves 2

↓

**mixed
berry–tofu**
smoothie

PER SERVING 190 CALORIES
● ● ● ●

hydrating

Made with coconut water, cucumber, romaine, and fresh fruit, these drinks will quench your thirst—and supply essential nutrients, too.

combine in a blender:

2 cups chopped honeydew

1 cup chopped English cucumber

12 fresh mint leaves

2 to 4 tablespoons lime juice, to taste

1 teaspoon honey

serves 2

↓

melon-mint
smoothie

PER SERVING 86 CALORIES
● ● ●

combine in a blender:

2 cups chopped mango

2 cups coconut water

2 to 3 tablespoons lime juice, to taste

Pinch of cayenne pepper

serves 2

↓

mango–coconut water smoothie

PER SERVING 158 CALORIES
● ● ● ●

combine in a juicer:

1 peeled, cored, and chopped pear

1 chopped cucumber

3 chopped celery stalks

1-inch piece fresh ginger, peeled and chopped

serves 1

↓

cucumber-pear juice

PER SERVING 165 CALORIES
● ● ● ●

combine in a juicer:

2 cups chopped
watermelon

1 tablespoon lemon juice

1 teaspoon grated
lemongrass

½ teaspoon grated
peeled fresh ginger

Pinch of salt

serves 2

↓

watermelon-
ginger juice

PER SERVING 49 CALORIES
● ● ● ●

combine in a blender:

1 cup unsweetened
aloe-vera juice

1 cup chopped mango

½ cup ice

¼ cup orange juice

2 tablespoons
lemon juice

2 tablespoons honey

1 teaspoon grated
peeled fresh ginger

serves 2

↓

aloe-vera,
ginger, and
orange smoothie

PER SERVING 182 CALORIES
● ● ●

combine in a juicer:

5 cups chopped romaine

3 cups chopped
pineapple

1 cup baby spinach

serves 1

↓

pineapple-
spinach juice

PER SERVING 276 CALORIES
● ● ● ●

recharge

---

load up on your vegetables

Building in your vegetable intake at the midday meal means you're that much closer to meeting the right quota. These soups, salads, and other meat-free dishes will provide sustenance and nutrients galore.

roasted vegetables
with quinoa

Make this dish when butternut squash and brussels sprouts are in abundance. The tahini and mixed-herb sauce is delicious and versatile: Any extra is great on salads or as a dip for raw vegetables. *Serves 2*

½ butternut squash, peeled and diced

20 brussels sprouts, trimmed and halved

¼ cup melted coconut oil or extra-virgin olive oil

Coarse salt and freshly ground pepper

1 teaspoon smoked paprika (pimenton)

¾ cup plus 2 tablespoons water

½ cup quinoa, rinsed and drained

1 garlic clove

2 tablespoons tahini

3 tablespoons apple cider vinegar

¼ cup snipped fresh chives

¼ cup chopped fresh flat-leaf parsley leaves

¼ cup chopped fresh cilantro leaves

2½ cups baby spinach

Preheat oven to 425°F. On a rimmed baking sheet, toss squash and brussels sprouts with 2 tablespoons oil; season with salt and the paprika. Roast vegetables, tossing halfway through, until golden and tender, 25 to 30 minutes.

Meanwhile, bring ¾ cup water, the quinoa, and a pinch of salt to a boil in a medium saucepan. Reduce heat, cover, and simmer until liquid has been absorbed and quinoa is tender but still chewy, about 15 minutes. Transfer to a bowl; fluff with a fork.

Pulse garlic, tahini, vinegar, remaining 2 tablespoons oil, remaining 2 tablespoons water, the chives, parsley, and cilantro in a food processor until smooth. Season with salt and pepper. (Vegetables and sauce can be refrigerated, in separate airtight containers, up to 3 days.)

In a bowl, toss roasted vegetables with quinoa and 2 tablespoons sauce. Toss each serving with spinach, and season with salt and pepper.

VEGAN DAIRY-FREE NUT-FREE GLUTEN-FREE

PER SERVING 722 CALORIES, 39 G FAT (5 G SATURATED FAT), 0 MG CHOLESTEROL, 92 G CARBOHYDRATES, 17 G PROTEIN, 20 G FIBER

fennel, sunchoke, and green apple salad

Although also known as Jerusalem artichoke, the sunchoke is not a type of artichoke at all, but rather the tuberous root of a species of sunflower. Raw sunchoke has a mellow, earthy flavor and a crisp texture similar to jicama. We like it sliced thin and tossed with apple, fennel, and celery (all A-list antioxidants) and a lemony vinaigrette. *Serves 6*

1   bulb fennel, trimmed and thinly sliced, fronds reserved for garnish

4   large celery stalks, thinly sliced, ¼ cup inner leaves chopped

1   large sunchoke, peeled and thinly sliced

1   large Granny Smith apple, peeled, cored, and thinly sliced

3   tablespoons plus 1 teaspoon fresh lemon juice

2   tablespoons plus 1 teaspoon Dijon mustard

1   garlic clove, minced

2   teaspoons honey

¼   cup plus 2 tablespoons extra-virgin olive oil

    Coarse salt and freshly ground pepper

½   cup walnuts, toasted (see page 314) and coarsely chopped

Place fennel, celery, sunchoke, and apple in a bowl of cold water. Stir in 1 tablespoon lemon juice and refrigerate (to crisp them and prevent discoloration).

In another bowl, whisk together remaining 2 tablespoons plus 1 teaspoon lemon juice, the mustard, garlic, and honey. Whisk in oil until emulsified, and season with salt and pepper.

Drain chilled celery mixture, and dry in a salad spinner or blot with a paper towel; transfer to a serving bowl. Add celery leaves and walnuts. Toss with dressing, and garnish with fennel fronds.

DAIRY-FREE GLUTEN-FREE

PER SERVING 247 CALORIES, 19 G FAT (2 G
SATURATED FAT), 0 MG CHOLESTEROL, 17 G
CARBOHYDRATES, 3 G PROTEIN, 3 G FIBER

watercress
and potato soup

Watercress is one of the best sources of antioxidant vitamins A and C, making it a nutritional superstar—and an excellent reason to prepare this super-simple curative tonic (which happens to be delicious pureed, too). It is just right for a detoxifying routine, or any time you want to purify your diet even a little. *Serves 2*

1 tablespoon plus 1 teaspoon olive oil

3 garlic cloves, thinly sliced

1 large white potato, peeled and cut into ½-inch cubes

   Coarse salt and freshly ground pepper

3 cups chicken stock, preferably homemade (see recipe, page 314)

1½ cups water

2 bunches watercress, trimmed and coarsely chopped

   Lemon wedges, for serving

Heat oil in a medium saucepan over medium-high. Add garlic and cook until sizzling and fragrant, about 1 minute. Stir in potato and ½ teaspoon salt; cook 1 minute.

Add stock and the water, and bring to a boil. Reduce to a simmer, and cook until potatoes are tender, about 5 minutes. Stir in watercress, and simmer until just wilted, about 1 minute. Season with salt and pepper. Squeeze with lemon before serving.

DAIRY-FREE **NUT-FREE** GLUTEN-FREE

PER SERVING 101 CALORIES, 4 G FAT (1 G
SATURATED FAT), 0 MG CHOLESTEROL, 13 G
CARBOHYDRATES, 5 G PROTEIN, 1 G FIBER

PER SERVING 202 CALORIES, 8 G FAT (2 G
SATURATED FAT), 4 MG CHOLESTEROL, 26 G
CARBOHYDRATES, 8 G PROTEIN, 6 G FIBER

farro, pea shoot, and goat cheese salad

Keep this simple salad in mind throughout spring and early summer when fresh peas and their shoots can be found at farmers' markets—that's when they're at their sweetest and most tender. The rest of the year you can substitute frozen peas for fresh and spinach or watercress for the shoots. *Serves 6*

1   cup farro

    Coarse salt and freshly ground pepper

1   cup fresh shelled peas (from 1 pound peas in pods)

2   ounces pea shoots, torn into bite-size pieces

⅓   cup small fresh mint leaves

⅓   cup almonds, toasted (see page 314) and chopped

1   teaspoon finely grated lemon zest

1   tablespoon plus 1 teaspoon fresh lemon juice

1   tablespoon extra-virgin olive oil

¼   cup fresh goat cheese, crumbled (1 ounce)

Place farro in a medium saucepan, and cover with 4 inches of water; add a pinch of salt. Bring to a boil; reduce heat and simmer until tender, 30 to 35 minutes. Drain and transfer to a bowl; let cool completely.

Meanwhile, cook peas in a small saucepan of salted boiling water until tender, about 2 minutes. Drain and run under cold water to stop the cooking.

Add peas, pea shoots, mint, almonds, and lemon zest to farro. Toss with lemon juice and oil. Season with salt and pepper. Serve topped with goat cheese.

cucumber and yogurt soup

Fresh horseradish, available in spring and early fall, makes all the difference in this five-ingredient soup. Look for small, hard roots with no signs of sprouting, and grate it with a rasp-style grater, as you would fresh ginger. *Serves 2*

Cut 2 small seedless **cucumbers** into large chunks. Puree half the cucumber with 1½ cups **plain yogurt,** finely grated zest of 2 **lemons,** and 2 tablespoons finely grated peeled fresh **horseradish** in a blender until just smooth. Add remaining cucumber, and pulse just until chunky. Season with freshly ground **pepper.** Refrigerate until cold, about 1 hour. Stir soup well, and garnish with more grated lemon zest and thinly sliced cucumber, if desired.

NUT-FREE GLUTEN-FREE

PER SERVING 304 CALORIES, 5 G FAT (1 G SATURATED FAT), 108 MG CHOLESTEROL, 48 G CARBOHYDRATES, 18 G PROTEIN, 11 G FIBER

beet and buttermilk soup

This no-cook soup (an easy take on borscht) is chock-full of health-boosting properties: Red beets fight inflammation and support detoxification; buttermilk contains probiotics, which help maintain a healthy digestive tract. *Serves 4*

Puree 1 pound **beets,** peeled and chopped; 4 **scallions,** trimmed and chopped; and 3 cups **buttermilk** in a blender until smooth. Season with **coarse salt.** Refrigerate until cold, about 1 hour. Stir well. Serve soup swirled with more buttermilk, if desired.

NUT-FREE GLUTEN-FREE

PER SERVING 127 CALORIES, 2 G FAT (1 G SATURATED FAT), 7 MG CHOLESTEROL, 21 G CARBOHYDRATES, 8 G PROTEIN, 4 G FIBER

NUT-FREE GLUTEN-FREE

PER SERVING 198 CALORIES, 17 G FAT (4 G
SATURATED FAT), 217 MG CHOLESTEROL, 3 G
CARBOHYDRATES, 9 G PROTEIN, 1 G FIBER

swiss chard
salad with
poached egg

Swiss chard replaces romaine lettuce in this riff on Caesar salad, which features a garlic-anchovy vinaigrette. Each serving is topped with a poached egg and a small amount of Parmigiano-Reggiano, for maximum effect. *Serves 4*

1 garlic clove, minced

4 anchovies, minced

1 teaspoon Dijon mustard

2 tablespoons white-wine vinegar

3 tablespoons extra-virgin olive oil

Coarse salt and freshly ground pepper

4 large eggs

6 cups thinly sliced Swiss chard

2 tablespoons grated Parmigiano-Reggiano cheese (½ ounce)

Combine garlic, anchovies, mustard, and vinegar in a bowl. Add oil in a slow, steady stream, whisking until emulsified. Season with salt and pepper.

Bring 3 inches of water to a simmer in a skillet. Crack one egg at a time into a teacup or small bowl and gently slide into water. Cook until whites are just set and yolks are still loose, 3 to 4 minutes. Remove eggs from water using a slotted spoon. Season with salt and pepper.

Toss chard with vinaigrette, and divide among plates. Top each with a poached egg and cheese. Serve immediately.

baked sweet
potato with greens

Low in calories and high in fiber, sweet potatoes offer tremendous nutritional value. Here, they're topped with sautéed Swiss chard and sliced avocado, though you can try other vegetable toppings, depending on what's in season. *Serves 2*

2 sweet potatoes, scrubbed and pricked all over with a fork

1 tablespoon extra-virgin olive oil

1 small onion, thinly sliced

1 bunch Swiss chard, tough stems trimmed and leaves chopped

Coarse salt

1 avocado, halved, pitted, peeled, and sliced

Cayenne pepper

Lemon wedges, for serving

Preheat oven to 400°F. Bake sweet potatoes on a baking sheet until tender, about 45 minutes.

Meanwhile, heat oil in a large skillet over medium. Add onion and cook until tender, stirring occasionally, about 6 minutes. Add chard and cook, stirring, until bright green and wilted, about 5 minutes. Season with salt.

Split potatoes and top each with the greens and sliced avocado. Season with cayenne and salt. Squeeze with lemon before serving.

VEGAN DAIRY-FREE **NUT-FREE GLUTEN-FREE**

PER SERVING 363 CALORIES, 21 G FAT (3 G SATURATED FAT), 0 MG CHOLESTEROL, 43 G CARBOHYDRATES, 7 G PROTEIN, 13 G FIBER

quinoa salad
with zucchini, mint, and pistachios

What's not to love about this light, bright, refreshing salad? To make it, cooked quinoa is tossed with sautéed zucchini, roasted pistachios, fresh mint—and a good amount of lemon zest and juice. Pack it up for a picnic or lunch on the go. *Serves 4*

1½ cups water

1 cup quinoa, rinsed and drained

Coarse salt and freshly ground pepper

2 tablespoons extra-virgin olive oil

1 zucchini, thinly sliced

1 garlic clove, thinly sliced

3 scallions, thinly sliced

¼ cup roasted salted pistachios, chopped

Grated zest and juice of 1 lemon

½ cup packed fresh mint leaves, chopped, plus more for garnish

Bring the water, quinoa, and salt to a boil in a medium saucepan. Reduce heat, cover, and simmer until liquid has been absorbed and quinoa is tender but still chewy, about 15 minutes. Transfer to a large bowl; then fluff with a fork and let cool.

Heat oil in a large skillet over medium-high. Add zucchini; cook, stirring occasionally, until tender and golden, about 7 minutes. Add garlic; cook until fragrant (do not let brown), about 30 seconds. Season with salt and pepper, and add to quinoa.

Stir in scallions, pistachios, lemon zest and juice, and mint. Season with salt and pepper and serve.

VEGAN DAIRY-FREE GLUTEN-FREE

PER SERVING 286 CALORIES, 13 G FAT (2 G
SATURATED FAT), 0 MG CHOLESTEROL, 36 G
CARBOHYDRATES, 8 G PROTEIN, 5 G FIBER

PER SERVING 180 CALORIES, 7 G FAT (2 G
SATURATED FAT), 212 MG CHOLESTEROL, 19 G
CARBOHYDRATES, 11 G PROTEIN, 4 G FIBER

dashi-poached
sweet potatoes
and greens

Kombu—a deeply flavored dried seaweed—and dried mushrooms are simmered in water to develop the rich broth called dashi, here enriched with miso. A poached egg tops each serving of soup. *Serves 4*

1 (3-by-12-inch) kombu sheet, broken in half

3 dried shiitake mushrooms

2 quarts water

2 tablespoons shiro (white) miso paste

1 large sweet potato, peeled, halved, and cut into 1-inch pieces

   Coarse salt and freshly ground pepper

4 cups lightly packed tender greens, such as baby bok choy, tatsoi, or spinach

8 ounces silken tofu, drained and cut into 1-inch pieces

4 large eggs

Bring kombu, mushrooms, and the water to a boil in a large Dutch oven or stockpot. Reduce heat and simmer for 20 minutes. Discard kombu. Transfer mushrooms to a cutting board with a slotted spoon; let cool slightly, thinly slice, and return to pot.

Whisk in miso. Add sweet potato, and cook at a steady simmer (do not let boil) until fork-tender, about 15 minutes. Season with salt. Remove from heat, and stir in greens. Gently add tofu, trying not to break pieces.

Bring 3 inches of water to a simmer in a skillet. Crack one egg at a time into a teacup or small bowl, and gently slide into water. Cook until whites are just set and yolks are still loose, 3 to 4 minutes. Remove eggs from water using a slotted spoon. Season with salt and pepper.

Top soup with a poached egg and serve immediately.

squash salad
with tomatoes, zucchini blossoms, and ricotta

This peak-of-summer salad depends on finding the ripest, freshest ingredients. Look for squash blossoms at a farmers' market or specialty-food store, or simply replace them with a leafy green such as spinach. Bruising the thyme helps release its aromatic oils. *Serves 2*

1 generous handful thyme sprigs

½ cup extra-virgin olive oil

½ teaspoon finely grated lemon zest, plus 2 teaspoons fresh lemon juice

2 baby zucchini, thinly shaved lengthwise on a mandoline

4 baby pattypan squashes (a mixture of yellow and green), thinly shaved on a mandoline

4 ounces mixed teardrop or halved cherry small tomatoes (1 cup)

6 zucchini blossoms, halved or quartered if large

¼ cup fresh basil leaves, torn if large, plus more for garnish

Pinch of red-pepper flakes

¼ teaspoon coarse salt

Freshly ground black pepper

3 ounces fresh ricotta

On a cutting board, bruise thyme with the dull edge of a knife. Heat thyme and oil in a small saucepan over medium until small bubbles appear. Turn off heat and steep, covered, 20 minutes. Discard sprigs, leaving loose thyme leaves in oil. Whisk together lemon zest and juice and 2 tablespoons thyme oil (reserve remaining oil for another use; it can be refrigerated up to 2 weeks).

Combine half the dressing with the zucchini, pattypan squashes, tomatoes, zucchini blossoms, basil, red-pepper flakes, and salt. Season with black pepper and toss. Divide half the salad between 2 plates, and dot with half the ricotta. Top with remaining salad and remaining ricotta. Drizzle with remaining dressing, garnish with basil, and serve.

NUT-FREE GLUTEN-FREE

PER SERVING 216 CALORIES, 60 G FAT (10 G
SATURATED FAT), 13 MG CHOLESTEROL, 27 G
CARBOHYDRATES, 14 G PROTEIN, 8 G FIBER

broccoli and brown rice salad with pumpkin seeds

It's easy to incorporate more seeds—and their protein and healthy fats—into meals, beyond simply as a garnish for soups and salads. Here, pumpkin seeds are roasted with broccoli, then served over brown rice; a little grated Pecorino goes a long way as a garnish. *Serves 4*

1½ cups water

¾ cup short-grain brown rice

Coarse salt and freshly ground pepper

1 head broccoli (2 pounds), trimmed and cut into ½-inch-thick pieces

⅓ cup raw hulled pumpkin seeds (pepitas)

3 tablespoons olive oil

2 tablespoons finely grated Pecorino Romano cheese

Lemon wedges, for serving

Bring the water, rice, and salt to a boil in a medium saucepan. Reduce heat, cover, and simmer until grains are tender and water has been absorbed, 40 to 50 minutes. Remove from heat; let stand 10 minutes, then fluff with a fork.

Meanwhile, preheat oven to 425°F. On 2 rimmed baking sheets, drizzle broccoli and pumpkin seeds with oil. Season with salt and pepper. Toss to combine, then spread in a single layer. Roast, rotating sheets halfway through, until broccoli is golden and just tender, about 20 minutes. Let cool slightly.

Sprinkle broccoli with Pecorino, and serve over rice, with lemon wedges.

NUT-FREE GLUTEN-FREE

PER SERVING 514 CALORIES, 20 G FAT (3 G
SATURATED FAT), 2 MG CHOLESTEROL, 71 G
CARBOHYDRATES, 16 G PROTEIN, 9 G FIBER

VEGAN DAIRY-FREE

PER SERVING 683 CALORIES, 36 G FAT (6 G SATURATED FAT), 0 MG CHOLESTEROL, 70 G CARBOHYDRATES, 31 G PROTEIN, 22 G FIBER

barley with brussels sprouts, spinach, and edamame

Unlike pearl barley, the most common form of the grain, the hulled variety (also called barley groats) has only the outermost hull removed, making it nutritionally superior and slightly chewier. It takes only a bit longer to cook. Barley, brussels sprouts, ginger, edamame, and cashews make this complex dish a nutritional powerhouse. *Serves 2*

2   cups water

½   cup hulled barley (or barley groats)

    Coarse salt

1   cup frozen shelled edamame, thawed

2   tablespoons coconut oil or extra-virgin olive oil

1   tablespoon minced peeled fresh ginger

1   garlic clove, minced

½   pound small brussels sprouts (about 10), trimmed and thinly sliced

1   bunch spinach (about 1 pound), stems removed

½   cup cashews, coarsely chopped

    Red-pepper flakes

Bring the water, barley, and a pinch of salt to a boil in a medium saucepan. Reduce heat, cover, and simmer until grains are just tender, about 40 minutes. Add the edamame, stir, and cover; continue cooking until barley is tender and edamame is bright green, about 5 minutes more. Remove from heat, and let stand 10 minutes. Fluff barley with a fork.

Heat 1 tablespoon oil in a large skillet over medium. Add ginger and garlic; cook, stirring, until fragrant, about 1 minute. Add brussels sprouts and cook, stirring, until bright green and tender, about 2 minutes.

Make room in center of pan, and add remaining tablespoon oil, spinach, and cashews; cook, stirring, until spinach has wilted, about 2 minutes. Stir in barley and edamame. Season with salt and red-pepper flakes and serve.

buckwheat noodles, bok choy, and sweet potatoes in miso-lime broth

A well-stocked pantry makes this ultra-healthy soup come together quickly—all you need to shop for are shiitakes and bok choy. It's worth keeping miso on hand for other Asian-inspired meals; this recipe calls for shiro (white) miso, which is sweeter and milder than other types of miso, though those can be used in its place. *Serves 4*

2 tablespoons extra-virgin olive oil

1 tablespoon grated peeled fresh ginger

4 scallions, whites and greens separated and thinly sliced

3 garlic cloves, minced

4 ounces shiitake mushrooms, stemmed and thinly sliced

1 sweet potato, peeled and cut into ½-inch cubes

6 cups water

4 ounces soba noodles

Coarse salt

2 heads baby bok choy, sliced into ½-inch-thick pieces

½ cup shiro (white) miso

1 tablespoon fresh lime juice, plus lime wedges for serving

Heat oil in a large saucepan over medium. Add ginger, scallion whites, and garlic; cook, stirring, until fragrant, about 2 minutes. Add shiitakes and cook, stirring occasionally, until tender, about 2 minutes. Add sweet potato, and toss to coat. Add the water, and bring to a boil. Reduce heat and simmer until sweet potatoes are tender, 6 to 8 minutes.

Meanwhile, cook soba in a large pot of salted boiling water until al dente, according to package directions. Drain and rinse under cold water.

Add bok choy to sweet-potato mixture, and cook until leaves are just wilted and stems are crisp-tender, about 2 minutes. Stir in cooked noodles. Remove from heat.

Remove 1 cup hot broth, and whisk with miso until smooth, then stir into soup. Add lime juice, and season with salt. Serve soup immediately with scallion greens and lime wedges.

VEGAN DAIRY-FREE NUT-FREE

PER SERVING 401 CALORIES, 9 G FAT (1 G
SATURATED FAT), 0 MG CHOLESTEROL, 72 G
CARBOHYDRATES, 17 G PROTEIN, 9 G FIBER

VEGAN DAIRY-FREE NUT-FREE

PER SERVING 420 CALORIES, 10 G FAT (1 G
SATURATED FAT), 0 MG CHOLESTEROL, 82 G
CARBOHYDRATES, 9 G PROTEIN, 9 G FIBER

roasted squash
with grains, grapes,
and sage

Acorn squash helps control portions: Use half as a "bowl," and it'll hold one of the daily-recommended servings of a cooked whole grain. Wheat berries, spelt, and barley are all good options here. A mixture of red and black grapes makes a pretty presentation, but you could use just one or the other. *Serves 4*

2½ cups water

½ cup wheat berries

Coarse salt and freshly ground pepper

2 acorn squash (about 1½ pounds each), halved lengthwise and seeded

2 tablespoons plus 1 teaspoon extra-virgin olive oil

1 pound mixed black and red grapes (about 3 cups)

1 large shallot, thinly sliced

2 tablespoons packed small fresh sage leaves

Bring the water, wheat berries, and a pinch of salt to a boil in a medium saucepan. Reduce heat, cover, and simmer until grains are tender, 30 to 40 minutes. Drain off excess liquid.

Preheat oven to 400°F. Brush cut sides of squash halves with 1 teaspoon oil; season with salt and pepper. Place squash, cut sides down, on a rimmed baking sheet.

Combine grapes, shallot, and sage in a bowl, and drizzle with remaining 2 tablespoons oil. Season with salt and pepper. Arrange around squash. Roast, stirring grape mixture once, until squash is tender and grape mixture is caramelized, 35 to 40 minutes. Fill squash with wheat berries and the grape mixture. Serve immediately.

roasted sweet peppers and carrots with orange and hazelnuts

Getting your fill of beta-carotene is easy with this vibrant salad: Carrots and orange bell peppers are packed with it, and oranges and clementines are loaded with vitamin C—all are powerful antioxidants. *Serves 4*

2 orange bell peppers, halved, ribs and seeds removed

5 small carrots, halved lengthwise

2 tablespoons extra-virgin olive oil, plus more for drizzling

Coarse salt and freshly ground pepper

1 navel orange, peel and pith removed, sliced into rounds

1 clementine, peel and pith removed, sliced into rounds

¼ cup fresh goat cheese, crumbled (1 ounce)

¼ cup hazelnuts, toasted (see page 314) and chopped

1 tablespoon sherry vinegar

Preheat oven to 425°F. Spread peppers and carrots on a rimmed baking sheet. Drizzle with oil, and season with salt and pepper. Roast until golden brown and tender, tossing halfway through, about 20 minutes.

Arrange roasted carrots and peppers with orange and clementine on a platter. Top with goat cheese and hazelnuts.

In a bowl, whisk together vinegar and 2 tablespoons oil until emulsified; season with salt and pepper. Drizzle over vegetables and serve.

GLUTEN-FREE

PER SERVING 233 CALORIES, 16 G FAT (4 G
SATURATED FAT), 11 MG CHOLESTEROL, 19 G
CARBOHYDRATES, 6 G PROTEIN, 4 G FIBER

beet, avocado, and arugula salad with sunflower seeds

This super-detoxifying salad is part of the 3-Day Action Plan (although it merits being part of any regular meal rotation). Prepare the beet slaw on the first day, and refrigerate leftovers in a covered container. Add greens, avocado, and seeds just before eating. *Serves 3*

For the Beet Slaw

- 2 beets, peeled and grated or thinly sliced
- 4 celery stalks, thinly sliced
- 1 English cucumber, thinly sliced
- 2 scallions, green parts only, thinly sliced

For the Salad

- 3 cups baby arugula
- ¼ cup plus 2 tablespoons extra-virgin olive oil
- ¼ cup plus 2 tablespoons fresh lemon juice
- Coarse salt and freshly ground pepper
- 1½ avocados, pitted, peeled, and diced
- 3 tablespoons raw hulled sunflower seeds, toasted (see page 314)

Make the beet slaw: In a bowl, toss together beets, celery, cucumber, and scallions.

Make the salad: For each serving, toss 2 cups beet slaw with 1 cup arugula and 2 tablespoons each oil and lemon juice. Season with salt and pepper. Top with ½ avocado and 1 tablespoon seeds, and serve immediately.

VEGAN DAIRY-FREE **NUT-FREE** GLUTEN-FREE

PER SERVING 238 CALORIES, 19 G FAT (2 G
SATURATED FAT), 0 MG CHOLESTEROL, 16 G
CARBOHYDRATES, 5 G PROTEIN, 6 G FIBER

pureed **cauliflower soup**

Cauliflower puree is so naturally rich, there's no need to add any dairy to this "creamy" soup. You could even serve the puree on its own, with just a little extra-virgin olive oil and salt and pepper mixed in. Here, the leaves are roasted for a crispy garnish. When shopping for cauliflower, look for heads that are heavy and tight, with no brown spots. *Serves 4*

2½ cups chicken stock, preferably homemade (see recipe, page 314), plus more if needed

1 head cauliflower, cut into florets, plus 8 small leaves (or 2 large leaves, coarsely chopped) for garnish

Coarse salt and freshly ground pepper

¼ teaspoon extra-virgin olive oil

Preheat oven to 450°F. In a medium saucepan, combine stock and cauliflower; season with salt and pepper. Bring to a boil; then reduce to a simmer. Cover and cook until cauliflower is very tender, about 20 minutes. Puree soup with an immersion blender until smooth, adding more stock as needed to achieve desired consistency. (Or puree in a regular blender, working in batches so as not to fill jar more than halfway; reheat soup in pan, if desired.)

Meanwhile, toss cauliflower leaves with oil on a baking sheet; season with salt and pepper. Roast until browned, about 10 minutes.

Garnish soup with cauliflower leaves before serving.

DAIRY-FREE **NUT-FREE GLUTEN-FREE**

PER SERVING 80 CALORIES, 1 G FAT (0 G
SATURATED FAT), 0 MG CHOLESTEROL, 12 G
CARBOHYDRATES, 8 G PROTEIN, 5 G FIBER

brussels sprout salad with avocado and pumpkin seeds

The tender leaves of brussels sprouts make wonderful salad "greens." Look for very firm, tight sprouts—the smaller the sprout, the sweeter it will be—without any unblemished leaves (or simply remove those before separating the rest). Avocado adds creaminess and heft to the dish, toasted pepitas a bit of crunch. *Serves 6*

1 teaspoon finely grated lemon zest plus 1½ tablespoons lemon juice

½ teaspoon Dijon mustard

3 tablespoons extra-virgin olive oil

Coarse salt and freshly ground pepper

1 pound brussels sprouts, trimmed and leaves separated

2 tablespoons raw hulled pumpkin seeds (pepitas), toasted (see page 314)

1 avocado, halved, pitted, peeled, and sliced

Whisk together lemon zest and juice and mustard in a bowl. Add oil in a slow, steady stream, whisking until emulsified. Season with salt and pepper.

In another bowl, toss dressing with brussels sprout leaves and pumpkin seeds. Gently stir in avocado, season with salt and pepper, and serve immediately.

VEGAN DAIRY-FREE **NUT-FREE** GLUTEN-FREE

PER SERVING 166 CALORIES, 13 G FAT (2 G
SATURATED FAT), 0 MG CHOLESTEROL, 10 G
CARBOHYDRATES, 4 G PROTEIN, 5 G FIBER

NUT-FREE

PER SERVING 455 CALORIES, 25 G FAT (5 G SATURATED FAT), 9 MG CHOLESTEROL, 49 G CARBOHYDRATES, 16 G PROTEIN, 13 G FIBER

broccoli-spinach soup with avocado toasts

Tahini, a thick, creamy paste made from ground, toasted sesame seeds, is an essential component of hummus and baba ghanoush, and it adds silken texture to other dips and spreads as well as salad dressings and soups. It's rich in vitamins and minerals and high in protein. Look for it at natural-food stores and most supermarkets. *Serves 4*

1 tablespoon olive oil, plus more for drizzling

1 leek, white and light-green parts only, thinly sliced and rinsed well

4 cups chicken stock, preferably homemade (see recipe, page 314) or water, plus more if needed

1 head broccoli, trimmed and chopped

6 ounces baby spinach (6 cups)

⅓ cup grated Parmigiano-Reggiano

2 tablespoons tahini

Coarse salt and freshly ground pepper

4 slices rustic bread

2 avocados, halved, pitted, peeled, and sliced

¼ cup radish or broccoli sprouts

1 lemon, cut into wedges

Heat oil in a medium saucepan over medium-high. Add leek and cook until tender, stirring occasionally, about 4 minutes. Add stock and bring to a boil. Add broccoli and cook, covered, until bright green and tender, about 2 minutes.

Remove from heat. Stir in spinach, cheese, and tahini. Season with salt and pepper. Let cool slightly. Puree soup with an immersion blender until smooth, adding more stock as needed to achieve desired consistency. (Or puree in a regular blender, working in batches so as not to fill jar more than halfway; reheat soup in pan, if desired.)

Toast bread and top with avocado and sprouts. Season with salt and pepper, squeeze with lemon wedges, and drizzle with oil. Serve alongside soup.

DAIRY-FREE **NUT-FREE** GLUTEN-FREE

PER SERVING 334 CALORIES, 16 G FAT (2 G SATURATED FAT), 0 MG CHOLESTEROL, 42 G CARBOHYDRATES, 12 G PROTEIN, 7 G FIBER

roasted portobellos with kale and red onion

Portobellos, a mainstay of vegetarian cooking, offer a chewy texture and umami quality similar to that of red meat. Here, the generously sized mushroom caps are marinated, roasted, topped with sautéed kale, and sprinkled with red-pepper flakes. *Serves 2*

¼ cup apple cider vinegar

1 tablespoon honey

4 garlic cloves, 2 finely chopped, 2 thinly sliced

2 tablespoons extra-virgin olive oil

Coarse salt and freshly ground black pepper

4 portobello mushrooms, stems removed

½ small red onion, thinly sliced

Pinch of red-pepper flakes, plus more for serving

6 cups thinly sliced kale

Combine vinegar, honey, chopped garlic, and 1 tablespoon oil in a bowl. Season with salt and black pepper. Arrange mushrooms in a single layer on a parchment-lined rimmed baking sheet. Drizzle with vinaigrette, cover, and marinate, turning occasionally, at room temperature for at least 30 minutes (or overnight in the refrigerator).

Preheat oven to 400°F. Roast mushrooms, flipping once, until tender, about 30 minutes.

Meanwhile, heat remaining tablespoon oil in a large skillet over medium. Add red onion, sliced garlic, and red-pepper flakes. Cook, stirring, until onion is softened, about 5 minutes. Add kale and season with salt. Cook, covered, until bright green and tender, tossing once or twice, about 4 minutes.

Top roasted mushrooms with kale mixture, sprinkle with red-pepper flakes, and serve immediately.

white peach and heirloom tomato salad

Here's an excellent reason to visit a farm stand or to join a CSA (community-supported agriculture) group: This salad features just-picked peaches (white ones are shown here) and heirloom tomatoes, plus tender, fresh, flavorful basil. *Serves 4*

2 ripe white peaches, pitted and sliced

2 large heirloom tomatoes, sliced

¼ small red onion, thinly sliced

2 tablespoons fresh basil leaves, torn, plus sprigs for garnish

2 tablespoons crumbled ricotta salata

Coarse salt and freshly ground pepper

Extra-virgin olive oil, for drizzling

Arrange peach and tomato slices on a platter. Top with red onion, basil, and ricotta salata. Season with salt and pepper, drizzle with oil, and garnish with basil sprigs. Serve immediately.

NUT-FREE GLUTEN-FREE

PER SERVING 61 CALORIES, 2 G FAT (1 G
SATURATED FAT), 6 MG CHOLESTEROL, 10 G
CARBOHYDRATES, 2 G PROTEIN, 2 G FIBER

VEGAN DAIRY-FREE **NUT-FREE** GLUTEN-FREE

PER SERVING 498 CALORIES, 21 G FAT (3 G
SATURATED FAT), 0 MG CHOLESTEROL, 44 G
CARBOHYDRATES, 18 G PROTEIN, 15 G FIBER

cauliflower "rice" stir-fry with pumpkin seeds

Finely chopped cauliflower gives this dish a rice-like texture. Ginger and garlic are anti-inflammatories, while pumpkin seeds are rich in omega-3 fatty acids. Serve the stir-fry by itself or alongside a protein source, such as steamed black cod or poached chicken breast. *Serves 2*

½ head cauliflower (1 pound), cut into florets

2 tablespoons coconut oil or extra-virgin olive oil

1 small red onion, sliced

4 garlic cloves, minced

Coarse salt

¼ cup cleansing broth (page 314) or vegetable stock (page 314)

1 tablespoon minced peeled fresh ginger

1 thinly sliced small red chile

½ head broccoli (1 pound), cut into florets

1 large carrot, julienned

½ red bell pepper, diced

Juice of ½ lemon

2 tablespoons raw hulled pumpkin seeds (pepitas), toasted (page 314)

2 tablespoons fresh cilantro leaves

Pulse cauliflower florets in a food processor until finely chopped.

Heat 1 tablespoon oil in a large skillet over medium. Add half the red onion and half the garlic; cook, stirring, until tender, about 6 minutes. Add cauliflower and season with salt. Stir in broth; steam, covered, until broth has evaporated and cauliflower is tender, about 6 minutes. Transfer to a bowl, and cover to keep warm.

Wipe pan clean, and heat remaining tablespoon oil over medium-high. Add remaining onion; cook, stirring, until tender, about 5 minutes. Add remaining garlic, the ginger, and chile; cook 1 minute. Add broccoli florets, carrot, and bell pepper; cook, stirring, until tender, about 5 minutes. Season with salt. Remove from heat, and add lemon juice.

Top cauliflower with broccoli mixture. Sprinkle with pumpkin seeds and cilantro and serve.

bell pepper, yogurt, and harissa soup

Harissa, a North African blend of hot chiles, garlic, olive oil, and spices, adds fiery spice to dips, sauces, and marinades, as well as to this chilled yellow-pepper soup (the yogurt will tame the heat). Look for harissa (in tubes or jars) at Middle Eastern food markets or online vendors, or make it at home (see recipe, page 315). *Serves 4*

Puree 3 chopped **yellow bell peppers,** 2 teaspoons **harissa,** and 2 cups **plain yogurt** in a blender until smooth. Season with **coarse salt.** Refrigerate until cold, about 1 hour. Stir soup well, and serve garnished with finely diced bell pepper, if desired.

NUT-FREE GLUTEN-FREE

PER SERVING 91 CALORIES, 2 G FAT (1 G SATURATED FAT), 6 MG CHOLESTEROL,13 G CARBOHYDRATES, 6 G PROTEIN, 1 G FIBER

avocado, radish, and basil soup

Instead of combining these ingredients in a salad, puree them to make a bracing soup that's guaranteed to cool you off on a warm summer day. It features a full cup and a half of fresh basil, plus a pair of creamy avocados. *Serves 5*

Puree 2 halved, pitted, and peeled **avocados,** 3 cups cold **water,** 1½ cups fresh **basil** leaves, and 2 tablespoons fresh **lemon juice** in a blender until smooth. Season with **coarse salt.** Add 3 large **radishes,** trimmed and chopped, and pulse until chunky, about 4 times. Season with freshly ground **pepper.** Cover with plastic wrap, pressing directly onto surface; refrigerate until cold, about 1 hour. Stir soup well, and serve garnished with radish slices and whole basil leaves, if desired.

VEGAN DAIRY-FREE
NUT-FREE GLUTEN-FREE

PER SERVING 120 CALORIES, 11 G FAT (1 G SATURATED FAT), 0 MG CHOLESTEROL, 7 G CARBOHYDRATES, 2 G PROTEIN, 5 G FIBER

bulgur salad with pomegranate seeds

Pomegranate seeds and raisins make sweet additions to tabbouleh, which is really an herb salad with a little grain added (contrary to many American versions that reverse that ratio). The bulgur only needs to be soaked in cold water to become tender—no cooking required. *Serves 4*

1 cup cracked bulgur wheat

Coarse salt and freshly ground pepper

4 scallions, trimmed and thinly sliced on the bias

½ cup chopped fresh flat-leaf parsley leaves

½ cup chopped fresh mint leaves

⅓ cup golden raisins

1 cup pomegranate seeds

2 tablespoons fresh lemon juice

2 tablespoons extra-virgin olive oil

Place bulgur and 1 teaspoon salt in a bowl, and cover with hot water by 1 inch. Let stand until bulgur is tender and plumped, about 20 minutes; drain in a sieve.

Toss bulgur with scallions, parsley, mint, raisins, pomegranate seeds, lemon juice, and oil. Season with salt and pepper and serve.

VEGAN DAIRY-FREE **NUT-FREE**

PER SERVING 291 CALORIES, 7 G FAT (1 G
SATURATED FAT), 0 MG CHOLESTEROL, 53 G
CARBOHYDRATES, 7 G PROTEIN, 11 G FIBER

VEGAN DAIRY-FREE **NUT-FREE**

PER SERVING 227 CALORIES, 15 G FAT (2 G SATURATED FAT), 0 MG CHOLESTEROL, 19 G CARBOHYDRATES, 6 G PROTEIN, 6 G FIBER

roasted mushroom tartines with avocado

Roasting gives mushrooms a more intense, earthy flavor than sautéing. The mushrooms here are layered over mashed avocado atop whole-wheat bread to make tartines (French open-faced sandwiches). *Serves 4*

8 ounces mixed small shiitake and cremini mushrooms, stemmed and halved

2 tablespoons extra-virgin olive oil

Coarse salt and freshly ground pepper

1 teaspoon fresh lemon juice

1 avocado, halved, pitted, peeled, and mashed

4 slices whole-wheat bread, toasted

Lemon wedges, for serving

Preheat oven to 450°F. In a baking dish, toss mushrooms with oil; season with salt and pepper. Roast until soft and juicy, about 15 minutes.

Squeeze lemon over avocado, and season with salt. Divide among toasts, mashing with a fork, and top with roasted mushrooms. Serve the tartines with extra lemon wedges.

roasted golden-beet, avocado, and watercress salad

It's worth seeking out a bunch of baby golden beets to make this delightful salad, although you could use red or Chioggia beets instead (just increase the cooking time depending on their size). Goat cheese is a natural partner for beets, and a little (just one ounce) goes a long way. *Serves 4*

1 bunch (about 12 ounces) baby golden beets, trimmed and scrubbed

2 tablespoons extra-virgin olive oil

Coarse salt and freshly ground pepper

1 bunch (about 4 ounces) watercress, trimmed, large sprigs torn into pieces

2 radishes, trimmed and thinly sliced

1 avocado, halved, pitted, peeled, and sliced

1 tablespoon snipped fresh chives

1 teaspoon red-wine vinegar

¼ cup fresh goat cheese, crumbled (1 ounce)

Preheat oven to 425°F. Place beets on a piece of foil lined with parchment. Drizzle with 1 tablespoon oil, and season with salt and pepper. Fold parchment and foil into a packet and tightly seal. Roast on a rimmed baking sheet until beets are tender, about 45 minutes. Carefully open packet, let cool slightly, and then remove skin. Cut beets into wedges.

Combine beets, watercress, radishes, avocado, and chives on a platter. Season with salt and pepper. Whisk together vinegar and remaining tablespoon oil, and season with salt and pepper. Drizzle over salad and gently toss. Serve immediately, topped with goat cheese.

NUT-FREE GLUTEN-FREE

PER SERVING 202 CALORIES, 16 G FAT (4 G
SATURATED FAT), 6 MG CHOLESTEROL, 13 G
CARBOHYDRATES, 4 G PROTEIN, 6 G FIBER

VEGAN DAIRY-FREE **NUT-FREE** GLUTEN-FREE

PER SERVING 91 CALORIES, 4 G FAT (1 G
SATURATED FAT), 0 MG CHOLESTEROL, 13 G
CARBOHYDRATES, 4 G PROTEIN, 4 G FIBER

creamy summer squash soup with cilantro

Both forms of the coriander plant, known for its anti-inflammatory and cholesterol-lowering properties, are used in this soup: the green leaves, known as cilantro, and the ground seeds, which have a very different, citrusy taste. When using cilantro, don't overlook the stems; here, they are cooked along with the soup for extra flavor. *Serves 4*

1 tablespoon extra-virgin olive oil

1 onion, chopped

3 garlic cloves, chopped

¼ cup chopped fresh cilantro stems, plus ¼ cup chopped cilantro leaves for garnish

1 teaspoon ground coriander

5 yellow summer squash (2½ pounds), chopped

2½ cups water, plus more if needed

Coarse salt

Lime wedges, for serving

Heat oil in a medium saucepan over medium. Add onion and cook, stirring occasionally, until softened, about 5 minutes. Add garlic, cilantro stems, and coriander; cook, stirring, until fragrant, about 2 minutes. Add squash and the water, and bring to a boil. Reduce heat and simmer, covered, until squash is just tender, about 15 minutes. Season with salt.

Puree soup with an immersion blender until smooth, adding more water as needed to achieve desired consistency. (Or puree in a regular blender, working in batches so as not to fill jar more than halfway; reheat in pan if desired.) Season with salt. Garnish soup with cilantro leaves, and serve immediately with lime wedges.

farro and roasted sweet potato salad

You might not think of pairing farro with roasted sweet potatoes, but they make a delightful combination. Whole garlic cloves are roasted alongside the sweet potatoes, then mashed and added to the salad for an extra dose of sweet flavor—and antioxidants. *Serves 4*

2 pounds sweet potatoes (about 4), scrubbed and cut into 1-inch pieces

3 garlic cloves (do not peel)

¼ cup plus 1 tablespoon extra-virgin olive oil

Coarse salt and freshly ground pepper

1 cup farro

Grated zest and juice of 1 lemon (about 3 tablespoons)

½ cup fresh dill, chopped

½ cup spicy sprouts, such as radish or arugula, plus more for garnish

Preheat oven to 425°F. On 2 rimmed baking sheets, drizzle sweet potatoes and garlic with 3 tablespoons oil. Season with salt and pepper. Toss to combine, then spread in a single layer. Roast sweet potatoes, flipping once, until tender and caramelized, about 30 minutes.

Meanwhile, place farro in a medium saucepan, and cover with 4 inches of water. Bring to a boil; reduce heat and simmer until tender, 30 to 35 minutes. Drain and immediately toss with remaining 2 tablespoons oil in a bowl. Season with salt, and let cool slightly.

Remove garlic cloves from skins, and use a mortar and pestle (or a fork) to mash with lemon zest and juice. Add to farro along with sweet potatoes, dill, and sprouts, and toss to combine. Season with salt and pepper. Garnish with more sprouts before serving.

VEGAN DAIRY-FREE **NUT-FREE**

PER SERVING 505 CALORIES, 9 G FAT (3 G
SATURATED FAT), 0 MG CHOLESTEROL, 78 G
CARBOHYDRATES, 10 G PROTEIN, 12 G FIBER

white bean, potato,
and kale stew

This robust stew is Italian in spirit, from the combination of flavors to the economical use of water as the cooking liquid, thickened with the starch from the potatoes. Here's a tip: Save the rind whenever you are finished with a wedge of Parmigiano-Reggiano and toss it into a soup as it simmers to add more flavor (and reduce the need for salt). *Serves 6*

2 tablespoons extra-virgin olive oil

1 onion, finely chopped

2 garlic cloves, minced

2 carrots, finely chopped

2 celery stalks, finely chopped

   Coarse salt and freshly ground pepper

1 can (15 ounces) peeled whole tomatoes, chopped (juice reserved)

7 cups water

½ pound small red potatoes, scrubbed and quartered

2 cups cooked white beans (see page 54), drained and rinsed

1 bunch kale (1 pound), stems removed and leaves torn into small pieces

½ cup finely grated Parmigiano-Reggiano cheese (2 ounces)

Heat oil in a large saucepan over medium. Add onion, garlic, carrots, and celery; season with salt. Cook vegetables, stirring, until tender, about 8 minutes.

Increase heat to medium-high, and add tomatoes and their juice. Cook, stirring, until mixture begins to caramelize, about 3 minutes.

Add the water, potatoes, and beans; bring soup to a boil. Reduce heat and simmer until potatoes are tender, about 10 minutes. Stir in kale. Cook, covered, until tender, about 2 minutes. Season with salt and pepper.

Serve stew topped with cheese.

NUT-FREE GLUTEN-FREE

PER SERVING 254 CALORIES, 7 G FAT (2 G SATURATED FAT), 6 MG CHOLESTEROL, 38 G CARBOHYDRATES, 12 G PROTEIN, 8 G FIBER

PER SERVING 372 CALORIES, 27 G FAT (4 G
SATURATED FAT), 0 MG CHOLESTEROL, 30 G
CARBOHYDRATES, 7 G PROTEIN, 11 G FIBER

steamed vegetable salad with macadamia dressing

Sometimes the dressing makes the salad. This one is tart and sweet and crunchy, thanks to a combination of citrus juice, apple cider vinegar, honey, and toasted macadamia nuts, plus a generous helping of fresh herbs. The dressing can double as a dip for crudités. *Serves 2*

3 tablespoons fresh citrus juice (any combination of lime, lemon, and orange)

1 teaspoon apple cider vinegar

½ teaspoon honey

2 tablespoons extra-virgin olive oil

1½ tablespoons chopped fresh dill, plus sprigs for garnish

1½ tablespoons chopped fresh flat-leaf parsley leaves, plus whole leaves for garnish

4 fresh basil leaves, sliced, plus whole leaves for garnish

¼ cup raw macadamia nuts, toasted (see page 314) and finely chopped

Coarse salt

½ large fennel bulb, trimmed and sliced ½ inch thick

½ pound asparagus, trimmed

¼ pound green beans, trimmed

½ pound small carrots, scrubbed

Whisk together citrus juice, vinegar, honey, oil, herbs, and nuts in a bowl, and season with salt.

Fill a pot with about 2 inches of water. Set a steamer basket or colander in pot. Bring water to a boil, then reduce to a simmer. Working in batches, steam vegetables, covered, until crisp-tender, 2 to 4 minutes; transfer to a cutting board. Halve steamed asparagus spears and carrots lengthwise.

Arrange vegetables on a platter, and season with salt. Drizzle vegetables with dressing, and garnish with herbs.

roasted red-pepper salad with anchovy white beans

Roasting your own red peppers is easy enough to do, and they are so much better than jarred varieties. Here, they are the main part of an antipasti-style salad, but you could also use them in salads or on sandwiches, or pureed into dips and spreads such as hummus. The anchovy dressing would also make a wonderful "house" dressing for green salads. *Serves 4*

4 small red bell peppers

Coarse salt and freshly ground pepper

2 anchovy fillets packed in olive oil, minced

1 garlic clove, minced

2 teaspoons sherry vinegar

3 tablespoons extra-virgin olive oil

¼ cup chopped fresh flat-leaf parsley leaves

1 can (15 ounces) small white beans, drained and rinsed

1 tablespoon grated Parmigiano-Reggiano cheese (¼ ounce)

1 cup packed spicy baby greens, such as watercress or arugula

Char bell peppers over the flames of a gas burner, turning with tongs until blackened and blistered, about 10 minutes. (Alternatively, broil them 2 or 3 inches from heat source.) Transfer peppers to a bowl, cover with a plate, and let stand until cool. Scrape off skins with a paring knife, and wipe flesh clean with a paper towel. Keeping stems intact, cut peppers in half lengthwise, then remove and discard seeds. Arrange on a platter, and season with salt and pepper.

Whisk together anchovies, garlic, vinegar, oil, and parsley in a bowl. Add beans and toss to coat. Season with salt and pepper. Spoon over peppers, top with cheese and greens, and serve.

NUT-FREE GLUTEN-FREE

PER SERVING 201 CALORIES, 12 G FAT (2 G
SATURATED FAT), 3 MG CHOLESTEROL, 22 G
CARBOHYDRATES, 8 G PROTEIN, 7 G FIBER

VEGAN DAIRY-FREE **NUT-FREE** GLUTEN-FREE

PER SERVING 254 CALORIES, 15 G FAT (2 G
SATURATED FAT), 0 MG CHOLESTEROL, 30 G
CARBOHYDRATES, 5 G PROTEIN, 10 G FIBER

carrot, spinach, and green bean soup with dill

Although this soup was designed for our 3-Day Action Plan, it is a soothing option year-round. Turmeric, a relative of ginger, is an especially rich source of curcumin, an antioxidant that fights inflammation. Like all spices, turmeric loses its punch over time; be sure to replenish it every six to twelve months. *Serves 3*

3 tablespoons extra-virgin olive oil

1 large onion, diced

7 carrots, diced

¼ teaspoon ground turmeric

1 tablespoon coarse salt

10 cups water

8 ounces green beans, trimmed and cut into ½-inch pieces

3 packed cups baby spinach

3 tablespoons chopped fresh dill

3 lemons, halved

Heat oil in a large saucepan over medium. Add onion and cook, stirring occasionally, until soft, about 6 minutes. Stir in carrots, turmeric, and salt. Add the water, bring to a boil, then simmer until carrots are just tender, 30 minutes. Add beans and cook until just tender, about 2 minutes.

For each serving, place one third spinach and dill in a bowl; ladle 3 cups hot soup over greens, cover with a plate, and let steep 5 minutes. Squeeze with 1 lemon and serve.

reenergize

---

choose your snacks wisely

Treat the mid-morning or afternoon break with the same level of consideration as you do each meal. It's essential to keeping energy levels on an even keel. You never know when or where hunger may strike, so plan ahead (make big batches) and carry along any of these healthful snacks.

roasted **cauliflower**
yogurt dip

spicy
any-bean dip

roasted **beet**–
white bean
hummus

red pepper
and **walnut dip** with
pomegranate

roasted cauliflower yogurt dip

Roasted cauliflower has a deep, caramelized flavor; pureed with yogurt, it makes a velvety dip for crunchy vegetables. The dip gets even better over time, so prepare it ahead if you can.

Preheat oven to 425°F. Cut 1 large head **cauliflower** (about 2 pounds) into florets, and place on a rimmed baking sheet. Drizzle with 2 tablespoons **extra-virgin olive oil,** sprinkle with ¼ teaspoon whole **cumin seeds,** and season with **coarse salt** and **red-pepper flakes.** Toss to combine, then spread in a single layer. Roast, tossing halfway through, until golden brown and tender, about 25 minutes. Let cool. Puree cauliflower, 1 cup **plain yogurt,** and 1 tablespoon fresh **lemon juice** in a food processor until smooth. Season with salt. Dip can be refrigerated in an airtight container up to 5 days. Garnish with more oil and red-pepper flakes, and serve with **crudités.** *Makes 1½ cups*

NUT-FREE GLUTEN-FREE

PER SERVING (¼ CUP) 139 CALORIES, 8 G FAT (2 G SATURATED FAT), 4 MG CHOLESTEROL, 12 G CARBOHYDRATES, 6 G PROTEIN, 4 G FIBER

spicy any-bean dip

As its name suggests, this dip can be made with any type of bean—garbanzo, black, azuki, or whatever variety you have on hand. They all provide a healthy dose of protein and fiber.

Heat 2 tablespoons **extra-virgin olive oil** in a small skillet over medium. Add 1 minced **garlic** clove and 1 tablespoon chopped **red onion;** cook until tender, stirring often, about 2 minutes. Add ½ teaspoon **ground cumin** and ⅛ teaspoon **chili powder;** stir to combine, and remove from heat. Pulse 1½ cups cooked **beans,** drained and rinsed (see page 54), in a food processor until chopped. Add onion mixture and ¼ cup **water,** and pulse to combine. Season with **coarse salt** and freshly ground **pepper.** Stir in 1 tablespoon chopped fresh **flat-leaf parsley** leaves. Dip can be refrigerated in an airtight container up to 5 days. Garnish with chopped parsley, and serve with **crudités.** *Makes 1½ cups*

VEGAN DAIRY-FREE
NUT-FREE GLUTEN-FREE

PER SERVING (¼ CUP PLUS 2 TABLESPOONS) 174 CALORIES, 6 G FAT (1 G SATURATED FAT), 0 MG CHOLESTEROL, 21 G CARBOHYDRATES, 5 G PROTEIN, 4 G FIBER

red pepper and walnut dip with pomegranate

Muhammara, a Middle Eastern dip made with red peppers and walnuts, traditionally includes pomegranate molasses, which can be hard to find, so we used a combination of pomegranate juice and dates (for sweetness) in this version.

Roast 3 **red bell peppers** (see page 314). Soak 4 pitted **dates** in hot water until softened, about 10 minutes; drain. Process peppers, dates, ½ cup **pomegranate juice,** ½ cup toasted **walnuts** (see page 314), and ½ teaspoon **red-pepper flakes** until smooth in a food processor. With machine running, slowly add 2 tablespoons **extra-virgin olive oil** until thoroughly combined. Season with **coarse salt** and freshly ground **black pepper.** Dip can be refrigerated in an airtight container up to 3 days. Garnish with **pomegranate seeds,** and serve with **toasted pita bread.**
Makes 1½ cups

VEGAN DAIRY-FREE

<u>PER SERVING</u> (¼ CUP) 252 CALORIES, 15 G FAT (2 G SATURATED FAT), 0 MG CHOLESTEROL, 30 G CARBOHYDRATES, 3 G PROTEIN, 5 G FIBER

roasted beet– white bean hummus

We prefer roasting beets, rather than boiling, for the best flavor. Besides giving this dip a standout color, beets (as are lemon and garlic) are powerful detoxifiers.

Preheat oven to 425°F. Roast 1 small **beet** (see page 170), and rub off skin. Chop beet, then puree with 1 cup cooked **white beans,** drained and rinsed (see page 54), 2 tablespoons fresh **lemon juice,** 1 chopped **garlic** clove, and 1 tablespoon **extra-virgin olive oil** until combined. Season with **coarse salt** and freshly ground **pepper.** Hummus can be refrigerated in an airtight container up to 3 days. Sprinkle with more pepper, and serve with **crudités.**
Makes 1½ cups

VEGAN DAIRY-FREE
NUT-FREE GLUTEN-FREE

<u>PER SERVING</u> (¼ CUP) 91 CALORIES, 5 G FAT (1 G SATURATED FAT), 0 MG CHOLESTEROL, 9 G CARBOHYDRATES, 3 G PROTEIN, 2 G FIBER

hard-cooked eggs with mustard

Whole-grain mustard and fresh herbs dress up ordinary hard-cooked eggs. Try topping them instead with a dusting of paprika or a dollop of wasabi paste.

Place 4 **large eggs** in a saucepan, and cover with water by 1 inch. Bring to a boil, then immediately remove pan from heat, cover, and let stand 13 minutes. Use a slotted spoon to transfer eggs to an ice-water bath to stop the cooking. (Unpeeled eggs can be refrigerated up to 1 week.) Peel eggs and cut in half. Top each half with 1 teaspoon **whole-grain mustard** and a fresh **flat-leaf parsley** leaf. *Makes 4*

DAIRY-FREE NUT-FREE GLUTEN-FREE

PER SERVING (1 EGG) 68 CALORIES, 5 G FAT (1 G SATURATED FAT), 187 MG CHOLESTEROL, 0 G CARBOHYDRATES, 6 G PROTEIN, 0 G FIBER

sardine salad with lemon and herbs

Sardines make a nice change of pace from tuna in salads; this one features a dressing of lemons, capers, and fresh herbs. You could forgo the tarragon in a pinch, but it brings a lot of flavor to the dish. Serve the salad atop greens, as here, or whole-grain crackers.

Whisk together 2 tablespoons **extra-virgin olive oil,** 1 teaspoon finely grated **lemon** zest, juice of 1 lemon, and 1 teaspoon **Dijon mustard** in a bowl until emulsified. Stir in 1 tablespoon **capers,** drained and rinsed; 2 **celery** stalks, finely diced; 2 tablespoons chopped fresh **flat-leaf parsley** leaves, and 1 tablespoon chopped fresh **tarragon** leaves. Gently fold in 2 cans (4.2 ounces each) olive-oil-packed **sardines,** drained, and season with **coarse salt** and freshly ground **pepper.** (Salad can be refrigerated in an airtight container up to 3 days.) Serve over **watercress** or other leafy greens. *Serves 2*

VEGAN DAIRY-FREE NUT-FREE GLUTEN-FREE

PER SERVING 399 CALORIES, 28 G FAT (4 G SATURATED FAT), 177 MG CHOLESTEROL, 3 G CARBOHYDRATES, 31 G PROTEIN, 1 G FIBER

warm spinach–white bean dip

Do spinach dip one better: Increase the fiber and protein content by adding white beans to the mix.

Preheat oven to 350°F. Place 5 ounces **baby spinach** (3 cups), rinsed and with water still clinging to leaves, in a large saucepan over medium heat. Cover and cook until wilted, stirring once, 4 to 6 minutes. Squeeze out excess liquid, then coarsely chop spinach.

Pulse 1 cup fresh **ricotta** and 1½ cups cooked **cannellini beans,** drained and rinsed (see page 54), in a food processor until smooth. Transfer to a bowl, and add 1 tablespoon snipped fresh **chives** and 1½ teaspoons finely grated **lemon zest.** Season with **coarse salt** and freshly ground **pepper.** Stir in spinach. Bake in a 1-quart baking dish until bubbling, about 30 minutes. Season with pepper. Serve warm with **crudités.** *Makes 3 cups*

NUT-FREE GLUTEN-FREE

PER SERVING (¼ CUP) 55 CALORIES, 2 G FAT (1 G SATURATED FAT), 6 MG CHOLESTEROL, 6 G CARBOHYDRATES, 4 G PROTEIN, 2 G FIBER

roasted edamame with cranberries

Edamame stars in this unconventional nut-free trail mix. The soybeans are roasted until they are crisp and golden before being tossed with the dried fruit.

Preheat oven to 425°F. On a rimmed baking sheet, drizzle 1 cup thawed frozen shelled **edamame** with 1 teaspoon **extra-virgin olive oil**; season with **coarse salt.** Toss to combine, then spread in a single layer. Roast, stirring occasionally, until crisp and golden, about 20 minutes. Transfer to a bowl and let cool. Add ¼ cup unsweetened **dried cranberries,** and toss to combine. Trail mix can be stored in an airtight container at room temperature up to 1 week. *Makes 1¼ cups*

VEGAN DAIRY-FREE
NUT-FREE GLUTEN-FREE

PER SERVING (¼ CUP) 67 CALORIES, 2 G FAT (0 G SATURATED FAT), 0 MG CHOLESTEROL, 7 G CARBOHYDRATES, 4 G PROTEIN, 2 G FIBER

kale chips with sesame seeds

Homemade kale chips are worth the effort. They are crisper (and more affordable) than the packaged variety, and you can tailor the seasonings. Try toasted sesame oil with tamari, or coconut oil with cumin, turmeric, and cayenne.

Preheat oven to 200°F. Remove stems from 1 bunch **kale,** and tear leaves into 2-inch pieces. In a bowl, toss kale with 2 tablespoons **extra-virgin olive oil,** 1 tablespoon fresh **lemon juice,** and ¼ cup **sesame seeds.** Season with **coarse salt,** and toss to evenly coat. Arrange kale in a single layer on 2 parchment-lined rimmed baking sheets. Bake 30 minutes. Remove from oven. Using a spatula, flip kale over. Continue baking until dry and crisp, 50 to 55 minutes. Let cool completely. Chips can be stored in an airtight container at room temperature up to 3 days. *Makes 2 cups*

VEGAN DAIRY-FREE
NUT-FREE GLUTEN-FREE

PER SERVING (1 CUP) 262 CALORIES, 23 G FAT (2 G SATURATED FAT), 0 MG CHOLESTEROL, 10 G CARBOHYDRATES, 6 G PROTEIN, 3 G FIBER

garlic-herb yogurt cheese

Making yogurt cheese is easy to do if you plan ahead (it needs to drain at least 8 hours). Reserve the whey (the liquid that has drained off) for blending into smoothies; it's a great source of protein, calcium, potassium, and riboflavin.

Fold a piece of cheesecloth twice to form a 4-layer, roughly 18-inch square. Place in a sieve set over a bowl, and spoon 1 quart **plain yogurt** into center. Gather corners and tie a piece of kitchen twine just above yogurt to form a tight bundle. Let drain in refrigerator at least 8 hours and up to 24 hours. Cut open cheesecloth. Transfer yogurt cheese to a bowl (reserve whey for another use). Stir in 3 tablespoons snipped fresh **chives,** 2 tablespoons chopped fresh **flat-leaf parsley** leaves, and ½ teaspoon minced **garlic.** Season with **coarse salt** and freshly ground **pepper.** Yogurt cheese can be refrigerated in an airtight container up to 2 weeks. Serve with **crudités** and **toasts.** *Makes 1¼ cups*

NUT-FREE GLUTEN-FREE

PER SERVING (¼ CUP PLUS 1 TABLESPOON) 157 CALORIES, 4 G FAT (3 G SATURATED FAT), 15 MG CHOLESTEROL, 18 G CARBOHYDRATES, 13 G PROTEIN, 0 G FIBER

baked
apple chips

No special equipment is required to make fruit chips at home—just an oven set to a low temperature. An adjustable-blade slicer will also make chips of uniform thickness, or just use a sharp chef's knife.

Preheat oven to 225°F. Slice 2 sweet **apples** (such as Gala, Honeycrisp, or Pink Lady) into ⅛-inch-thick rounds, then remove seeds. Arrange slices in a single layer on 2 parchment-lined baking sheets. Bake 1 hour 30 minutes. Remove from oven. Using a spatula, flip apple slices over. Continue baking until crisp, about 1 hour more. Let cool completely. Chips can be stored in an airtight container at room temperature up to 1 week. *Makes about 40*

VEGAN DAIRY-FREE
NUT-FREE GLUTEN-FREE

PER SERVING (20 CHIPS) 72 CALORIES, 0 G FAT (0 G SATURATED FAT), 0 MG CHOLESTEROL,19 G CARBOHYDRATES, 1 G PROTEIN, 4 G FIBER

spiced
pumpkin seeds

Pumpkin seeds are a concentrated source of protein; they're also an excellent source of anti-inflammatory omega-3 fatty acids. They are available whole, as shown opposite, or hulled (called pepitas). Either type will work in this recipe.

Preheat oven to 350°F. Spread 1 cup raw **pumpkin seeds** in a single layer on a rimmed baking sheet. Roast, tossing halfway through, 20 minutes. Remove from oven. Toss seeds with 1 tablespoon **extra-virgin olive oil,** 1 tablespoon **honey,** and a pinch each of **ground cinnamon, ground cumin,** and **cayenne pepper.** Season with **coarse salt** and freshly ground **black pepper,** toss to combine, then spread in a single layer. Roast, tossing halfway through, until golden, about 15 minutes. Transfer seeds to a bowl, stirring as they cool to prevent sticking. Pumpkin seeds can be stored in an airtight container at room temperature up to 1 week. *Makes 1 cup*

DAIRY-FREE NUT-FREE GLUTEN-FREE

PER SERVING (½ CUP) 317 CALORIES, 26 G FAT (5 G SATURATED FAT), 0 MG CHOLESTEROL, 10 G CARBOHYDRATES, 15 G PROTEIN, 3 G FIBER

tuna
and white
beans

Keep canned tuna and white beans in the cupboard, and you can quickly put together this protein-packed mini-meal whenever hunger strikes.

Flake 1 can (5 ounces) **water-packed chunk-light tuna,** drained; toss with ½ cup cooked **white beans,** drained and rinsed (see page 54), in a bowl. Drizzle with 2 teaspoons **extra-virgin olive oil** and 2 to 3 teaspoons fresh **lemon juice,** to taste. Season with **coarse salt** and freshly ground **pepper.** Gently toss to combine and serve. *Serves 2*

DAIRY-FREE NUT-FREE GLUTEN-FREE

PER SERVING 197 CALORIES, 7 G FAT (1 G SATURATED FAT), 30 MG CHOLESTEROL, 12 G CARBOHYDRATES, 21 G PROTEIN, 3 G FIBER

steamed
green beans
with lemon

Here's a simple solution for snack time: Steam a bunch of green beans (or broccoli or asparagus), then keep at the ready in portion-size packs in the refrigerator.

Set a steamer basket or colander in a pot filled with 2 inches of boiling water. Place 4 ounces trimmed **green beans** in basket, cover, and steam until bright green and crisp-tender, about 5 minutes. Transfer to an ice-water bath to stop the cooking; let cool completely, then drain and pat dry. Green beans can be refrigerated in an airtight container up to 5 days. To serve, drizzle with **extra-virgin olive oil,** squeeze with **lemon,** and sprinkle with flaky **sea salt** (such as Maldon). *Serves 4*

VEGAN DAIRY-FREE
NUT-FREE GLUTEN-FREE

PER SERVING 20 CALORIES, 1 G FAT (0 G SATURATED FAT), 0 MG CHOLESTEROL, 2 G CARBOHYDRATES, 1 G PROTEIN, 1 G FIBER

spicy yogurt and cucumber dip

green goddess dip

Think of this creamy dip as a variation on raita, the traditional Indian condiment.

Avocado (in lieu of sour cream or mayonnaise) is to thank for the silken texture of this healthy reinterpretation of a favorite salad dressing. Anchovies, among the best sources of omega-3 fatty acids, boost flavor and nutrients.

Peel and grate ½ **English cucumber;** let drain in a fine sieve set over a bowl for at least 20 minutes, pressing down on solids to extract liquid. Heat 1 tablespoon plus 1 teaspoon **safflower oil** in a skillet over medium-high. Add 2 teaspoons **curry powder;** cook, stirring, until oil is just beginning to bubble, about 45 seconds. Transfer to a bowl; let cool slightly. Stir in 2 cups **plain Greek yogurt,** the cucumber, ¼ cup chopped fresh **mango,** 1 teaspoon finely grated peeled **fresh ginger,** and ½ cup fresh **cilantro** leaves, chopped; season with **coarse salt** and freshly ground **pepper.** Refrigerate at least 1 hour (or up to 3 days in an airtight container). Serve with **crudités.** *Makes 2½ cups*

Scoop 1 ripe **avocado** into a food processor, and add 1½ cups **buttermilk,** 1 cup chopped fresh **herbs** (such as flat-leaf parsley, basil, chives, and tarragon), 2 **anchovies** (preferably salt-packed, and rinsed well), and 1 tablespoon plus 1 teaspoon **white-wine vinegar.** Season with **coarse salt** and freshly ground **pepper.** Pulse until smooth and combined. Transfer to a bowl, and refrigerate at least 1 hour (or up to 2 days), pressing plastic wrap directly on surface. Serve with **crudités.** *Makes 2 cups*

NUT-FREE GLUTEN-FREE

PER SERVING (⅓ CUP DIP WITH 1 PAPPADAM) 122 CALORIES, 2 G FAT (0 G SATURATED FAT), 0 MG CHOLESTEROL, 16 G CARBOHYDRATES, 8 G PROTEIN, 2 G FIBER

NUT-FREE GLUTEN-FREE

PER SERVING (¼ CUP DIP WITH 6 ENDIVE LEAVES) 65 CALORIES, 4 G FAT (1 G SATURATED FAT), 3 MG CHOLESTEROL, 6 G CARBOHYDRATES, 3 G PROTEIN, 3 G FIBER

watercress and **avocado** roll

Think of this as a super-easy summer roll, using cabbage instead of a rice-paper wrapper. You can also swap out the watercress with arugula and the mint with basil or cilantro; the avocado is essential.

Stir together 1 cup chopped trimmed **watercress** and ½ mashed ripe **avocado,** 1 julienned peeled **carrot,** and 10 fresh **mint** leaves. Season with **coarse salt.** Divide mixture between halves of a **cabbage** leaf, top with 1 julienned **carrot** and 10 fresh **mint** leaves. Roll up to enclose and serve immediately. *Serves 1*

VEGAN DAIRY-FREE
NUT-FREE GLUTEN-FREE

PER SERVING 178 CALORIES, 14 G FAT (2 G SATURATED FAT), 0 MG CHOLESTEROL, 15 G CARBOHYDRATES, 3 G PROTEIN, 8 G FIBER

frozen grapes and **kiwi**

Freezing transforms the texture of antioxidant-rich grapes, turning them into little frosty treats, for a change of pace (and you'll chew them more slowly, too).

Place 1 cup **seedless grapes** and 1 **kiwi,** peeled and sliced into 1-inch pieces, on a parchment-lined baking sheet. Freeze until solid, about 1 hour. Transfer to an airtight container, and freeze up to 1 month before serving. *Serves 1*

VEGAN DAIRY-FREE
NUT-FREE GLUTEN-FREE

PER SERVING 144 CALORIES, 1 G FAT (0 G SATURATED FAT), 0 MG CHOLESTEROL, 37 G CARBOHYDRATES, 2 G PROTEIN, 4 G FIBER

simple
roasted
cauliflower

Like other cruciferous vegetables, cauliflower is an excellent source of anti-inflammatory properties. Here, it's roasted for a simple snack, but it would also make a great side dish for chicken or fish.

Preheat oven to 425°F. Spread ½ head **cauliflower,** cut into florets, on a rimmed baking sheet. Drizzle with 1 tablespoon **extra-virgin olive oil,** and season with **coarse salt.** Toss to combine, then spread in a single layer. Roast, tossing halfway through, until golden brown and just tender, about 25 minutes. Sprinkle with **red-pepper flakes** and serve. *Serves 2*

VEGAN DAIRY-FREE
NUT-FREE GLUTEN-FREE

PER SERVING 100 CALORIES, 7 G FAT (1 G SATURATED FAT), 0 MG CHOLESTEROL, 8 G CARBOHYDRATES, 3 G PROTEIN, 4 G FIBER

roasted
radishes and
greens

Next time you buy a bunch of radishes, try roasting them— greens and all. After just fifteen minutes in the oven, the roots become tender and caramelized, the greens light and crisp.

Preheat oven to 375°F. Separate 1 bunch **radishes** and their greens; halve any large radishes. Divide radishes and greens between 2 rimmed baking sheets, then drizzle with 1 tablespoon **extra-virgin olive oil.** Season with **coarse salt** and freshly ground **pepper.** Toss to combine, then spread in a single layer. Roast, tossing occasionally, until radishes are tender and caramelized and greens are crisp, 15 to 20 minutes. Let cool before serving. *Serves 4*

VEGAN DAIRY-FREE
NUT-FREE GLUTEN-FREE

PER SERVING 61 CALORIES, 7 G FAT (1 G SATURATED FAT), 0 MG CHOLESTEROL, 0 G CARBOHYDRATES, 0 G PROTEIN, 0 G FIBER

sweet-potato chips

It's easier than you think—and healthier, too—to make your own chips. Simply toss very thin slices of sweet potatoes in oil, and bake until crisp and golden.

Preheat oven to 400°F. Using a mandoline or other adjustable-blade slicer, cut 1 peeled **sweet potato** into very thin slices. Divide between 2 rimmed baking sheets, drizzle with 1 tablespoon **extra-virgin olive oil,** and season with **ground cumin, paprika,** and **coarse salt.** Toss to combine, then spread in a single layer. Roast, flipping halfway through, until crisp and golden, 20 to 25 minutes. Serve warm or at room temperature. Chips can be stored in an airtight container at room temperature up to 2 days. *Makes 2 cups*

VEGAN DAIRY-FREE
NUT-FREE GLUTEN-FREE

PER SERVING (½ CUP) 63 CALORIES, 4 G FAT (1 G SATURATED FAT), 0 MG CHOLESTEROL, 7 G CARBOHYDRATES, 1 G PROTEIN, 1 G FIBER

apple with peanut butter and oats

Make this packable snack ahead of time: Sandwich the stuffed apple halves together, and slice into wedges just before eating.

Halve 1 **apple** and use a teaspoon to remove core. Stuff each half with 1 teaspoon all-natural **crunchy peanut butter.** Sprinkle with ½ teaspoon **old-fashioned rolled oats.** *Serves 1*

VEGAN DAIRY-FREE

PER SERVING 145 CALORIES, 6 G FAT (1 G SATURATED FAT), 0 MG CHOLESTEROL, 23 G CARBOHYDRATES, 3 G PROTEIN, 4 G FIBER

pureed pea dip with mint and lemon

Don't wait for the arrival of fresh peas in spring to make this lemony dip; frozen peas are just as nutritious and much more convenient. Peas are surprisingly high in protein; tahini (sesame seed paste) ups the protein even more.

Cook 3 cups frozen **green peas** (do not thaw) in a pot of boiling water until tender, about 1 minute. Use a slotted spoon to transfer to a colander, and run under cold water to stop the cooking. Let cool completely, then drain. Pulse peas with ¼ cup fresh **mint** leaves, finely grated zest and juice of 1 **lemon,** 1 **garlic** clove, 2 tablespoons **extra-virgin olive oil,** and 1 tablespoon **tahini** in a food processor until thick and combined. Season with **coarse salt** and freshly ground **pepper.** Drizzle with additional oil, and serve with **carrots.** Dip can be refrigerated in an airtight container up to 1 day. *Makes 2 cups*

VEGAN DAIRY-FREE
NUT-FREE GLUTEN-FREE

PER SERVING (½ CUP) 173 CALORIES, 9 G FAT (1 G SATURATED FAT), 0 MG CHOLESTEROL, 17 G CARBOHYDRATES, 6 G PROTEIN, 5 G FIBER

melon with feta and black pepper

A bit of tangy feta and cracked black pepper turn slices of honey-dew—or any other variety of melon—into a scrumptious snack.

Cut ¼ **honeydew melon** into 2 wedges. Crumble ¼ cup **feta** over the top, season with freshly ground **pepper,** and serve. *Serves 1*

NUT-FREE GLUTEN-FREE

PER SERVING 190 CALORIES, 8 G FAT (6 G SATURATED FAT), 33 MG CHOLESTEROL, 24 G CARBOHYDRATES, 7 G PROTEIN, 2 G FIBER

trail mix with toasted coconut

Make a big batch of this mix for an on-the-go snack. You can change up the combination, too: Think walnuts, dried cranberries, and pumpkin seeds; hazelnuts, dried cherries, and dark chocolate; or pecans, raisins, and sunflower seeds.

Combine ½ cup each shelled unsalted **pistachios,** chopped unsweetened **dried apricots,** toasted unsweetened **coconut flakes** (see page 314), and chopped toasted **almonds** (see page 314) in a bowl. Trail mix can be stored in an airtight container at room temperature up to 2 weeks. *Makes 2 cups*

dried fruit and nut bites

Use your favorite dried fruits (make sure they're unsweetened), nuts, and seeds to make these no-bake treats. They'll help you power through any energy slump.

Pulse 2 cups mixed unsweetened **dried fruit** in a food processor until finely chopped; transfer to a bowl. Pulse 2 cups **mixed raw nuts** and **seeds** until finely chopped, and add to dried fruit along with a pinch each of **ground cinnamon** and **coarse salt.** Knead mixture until it comes together; then form into 1-inch balls. Place ⅓ cup **sesame seeds** in a bowl. Roll each ball in sesame seeds to coat. Fruit and nut bites can be stored in an airtight container at room temperature up to 5 days. *Makes 20*

VEGAN DAIRY-FREE GLUTEN-FREE

PER SERVING (¼ CUP) 160 CALORIES, 12 G FAT (4 G SATURATED FAT), 0 MG CHOLESTEROL, 11 G CARBOHYDRATES, 4 G PROTEIN, 3 G FIBER

VEGAN DAIRY-FREE GLUTEN-FREE

PER SERVING (1 BITE) 135 CALORIES, 8 G FAT (1 G SATURATED FAT), 0 MG CHOLESTEROL, 14 G CARBOHYDRATES, 3 G PROTEIN, 3 G FIBER

restore

---

make meals
with substance

The end of the day is a particularly important time for mindfulness. Make the most of the evening meal by taking the time to truly savor what you are eating. What's more, be sure to give your body the restorative charge it needs with protein-packed dishes like the ones that follow.

soba with salmon and watercress

Think of this method of cooking salmon (called shallow poaching) as an easy alternative to steaming it in a basket, since you need only a basic skillet. Here, the fish is flaked and tossed with watercress, soba noodles, and a tangy (and probiotic!) buttermilk-chive-lemon dressing. *Serves 4*

Coarse salt and freshly ground pepper

2 skinless wild salmon fillets (about 5 ounces each)

8 ounces soba noodles (100 percent buckwheat flour)

½ cup buttermilk

1 tablespoon extra-virgin olive oil

1 teaspoon finely grated lemon zest, plus 1 tablespoon fresh lemon juice

2 tablespoons minced fresh chives

1½ cups trimmed watercress

Bring 2 inches of water and a pinch of salt to a boil in a large sauté pan over medium-low heat. Add salmon and poach at a low simmer until cooked through, 7 to 8 minutes. Remove fish and let cool slightly, then flake into large pieces.

Meanwhile, cook soba in a pot of boiling salted water until al dente, according to package directions. Drain and rinse under cold water.

In a bowl, whisk together buttermilk, oil, lemon zest and juice, and chives; season with salt and pepper. Add soba and toss to combine. Add watercress and salmon and gently toss to combine. Serve immediately, or refrigerate, covered, up to 2 hours.

NUT-FREE GLUTEN-FREE

DAIRY-FREE **NUT-FREE** GLUTEN-FREE

PER SERVING 267 CALORIES, 15 G FAT (2 G SATURATED FAT), 51 MG CHOLESTEROL, 10 G CARBOHYDRATES, 25 G PROTEIN, 2 G FIBER

chicken paillards
with squash and spinach

Most people reach for butternut squash or acorn squash, but there are other varieties worth exploring, including Japanese kabocha squash. With its slightly sweet flesh and edible skin (which also contains many nutrients), kabocha is especially good roasted; try it steamed, too. *Serves 4*

½ small kabocha squash, unpeeled, seeded, and cut lengthwise into ¾-inch slices

1 small red onion, sliced into wedges, root end attached

¼ cup extra-virgin olive oil

Coarse salt

4 boneless, skinless chicken breast halves (4 to 5 ounces each), butterflied

Red-pepper flakes

16 fresh sage leaves (from about 4 sprigs)

1 cup baby spinach leaves

Preheat oven to 425°F. Place squash and red onion on 2 rimmed baking sheets. Drizzle 2 tablespoons oil evenly over vegetable mixture, and season with salt. Toss to coat, then spread in a single layer. Roast until squash is tender, about 15 minutes.

Meanwhile, pound chicken to a ⅛- to ¼-inch thickness. Season with salt and red-pepper flakes. Heat remaining 2 tablespoons oil in a large skillet over medium-high. Fry sage until just crisp, about 1 minute; use a slotted spoon to transfer to paper towels to drain.

Working in batches, add chicken to pan; sauté until golden and cooked through, about 1 minute per side. Serve chicken topped with spinach, roasted vegetables, and fried sage.

grilled tofu with chimichurri on toast

Vegans, take heart: Here's an appealing dish for the grilling season. Pressed tofu is marinated in chimichurri—an Argentinian herb sauce that's usually served with steak—and then grilled with slices of whole-grain bread. Cucumbers and avocado round out the meal. *Serves 4*

¼ red onion, finely chopped

½ cup chopped fresh flat-leaf parsley leaves

⅓ cup extra-virgin olive oil, plus more for drizzling

¼ cup sherry vinegar

2 tablespoons chopped fresh oregano

1 tablespoon minced garlic

½ teaspoon red-pepper flakes

Coarse salt

1 avocado, thinly sliced

½ English cucumber, thinly sliced

Freshly ground black pepper

1 lemon, cut into wedges

15 ounces firm tofu, drained, cut into four pieces, and pressed (see page 314)

Canola or safflower oil, for grill

4 slices whole-grain bread

Combine red onion, parsley, oil, vinegar, oregano, garlic, and red-pepper flakes in a bowl; season with salt. Reserve ½ cup sauce for serving. Marinate tofu at room temperature in remaining sauce, basting occasionally, for 1 hour.

Combine avocado and cucumber in a bowl. Season with salt and black pepper. Squeeze lemon over salad, and drizzle with oil; gently toss to combine.

Heat a grill (or grill pan) to medium; lightly oil hot grates. Lightly brush bread on both sides with marinade. Grill until crisp, about 2 minutes per side. Grill tofu until lightly charred, about 4 minutes per side. Serve on bread drizzled with reserved sauce, and with avocado salad on the side.

VEGAN DAIRY-FREE NUT-FREE

PER SERVING 456 CALORIES, 29 G FAT (5 G SATURATED FAT), 0 MG CHOLESTEROL, 22 G CARBOHYDRATES, 16 G PROTEIN, 7 G FIBER

wild salmon, asparagus, and shiitakes in parchment

Take a cue from professional chefs and cook fish en papillote. This type of steaming yields moist and tender fish that takes on the flavors of the other ingredients. A bit of extra-virgin olive oil, salt, and pepper are mainstays, as is some type of acid—here lemon, elsewhere sliced tomatoes (see page 270). *Serves 4*

8 ounces shiitake mushrooms, stemmed and thinly sliced

8 ounces medium asparagus (about ½ bunch), trimmed and halved lengthwise

4 scallions, trimmed and thinly sliced

¼ cup extra-virgin olive oil

Grated zest of 1 lemon, plus wedges for serving

Coarse salt and freshly ground pepper

4 skinless wild salmon fillets (about 5 ounces each)

¼ cup water

Preheat oven to 400°F. Cut four 12-by-17-inch pieces of parchment. Fold each in half crosswise to make a crease, then unfold and lay flat.

Toss mushrooms, asparagus, and scallions with oil in a bowl. Sprinkle with lemon zest, and season with salt and pepper. Remove asparagus from mixture; divide evenly among parchment pieces, creating a bed of spears on one side of crease. Top each with 1 piece of fish, then with mushroom mixture. Drizzle each serving with 1 tablespoon water. Fold parchment over ingredients, creating a half-moon shape. Make small overlapping pleats to seal the open sides.

Bake on 2 rimmed baking sheets until packets are puffed, 9 minutes (fish should be partially opaque in the middle). Open packets, squeeze with lemon, and serve immediately.

DAIRY-FREE **NUT-FREE** GLUTEN-FREE

PER SERVING 378 CALORIES, 23 G FAT (3 G SATURATED FAT), 78 MG CHOLESTEROL, 12 G CARBOHYDRATES, 31 G PROTEIN, 3 G FIBER

NUT-FREE GLUTEN-FREE

PER SERVING 411 CALORIES, 11 G FAT (3 G
SATURATED FAT), 10 MG CHOLESTEROL, 59 G
CARBOHYDRATES, 17 G PROTEIN, 7 G FIBER

brown rice cakes with sautéed fennel, broccoli rabe, and ricotta

These savory cakes are crisp on the outside, chewy in the middle. Delicious on their own, they're even better as a base for all kinds of toppings—think vegetables, eggs, and cheese. *Serves 4*

2 tablespoons extra-virgin olive oil, plus more for drizzling

1 bulb fennel (about 1 pound with fronds), cored, stems cut lengthwise into ¼-inch-thick slices

   Coarse salt

3 garlic cloves, thinly sliced

⅔ cup water

1 pound broccoli rabe, trimmed

4 large egg whites

3 cups cooked short-grain brown rice (from about 1¼ cups uncooked; see page 51)

¼ teaspoon fennel seeds, toasted and coarsely ground

½ cup fresh ricotta

   Freshly ground pepper

⅓ cup fresh basil leaves, for garnish

Heat 1½ teaspoons oil in a large nonstick sauté pan over medium-high. Add fennel; season with salt. Reduce heat to medium; cook, tossing once, until golden, 6 to 7 minutes. Clear space in pan, and add ½ teaspoon oil and the garlic. Sauté, stirring, until golden, 1 to 2 minutes. Add ⅓ cup water, cover, and cook over low heat until fennel is tender, about 2 minutes. Raise heat to medium-high; add remaining ⅓ cup water and the broccoli rabe. Season with salt. Cover and cook, stirring once, until greens are tender, about 3 minutes more. Remove from heat and let sit, uncovered.

Heat 2 teaspoons oil in another large nonstick pan over medium-high. Whisk egg whites in a bowl until very foamy but not stiff. Stir in rice, fennel seeds, and ½ teaspoon salt. Drop 4 separate spoonfuls (about half the batter) into pan, and spread each into a 3-inch round. Cook until golden brown and set, 3 to 4 minutes. Flip; cook 1 minute more. Wipe pan clean, and repeat process with remaining 2 teaspoons oil and batter.

Divide cakes and ricotta among 4 plates, and top cakes with vegetables. Drizzle with oil, season with pepper, and garnish with basil. Serve immediately.

spicy indian chicken and tomato soup

The secret to success for most soups and stews lies in the stock; this one is made from a whole chicken and a handful of aromatics. You end up with a heady cooking liquid and more chicken than you need for the recipe (reserve the rest for salads). Toasting whole spices, another building block in many Indian preparations, helps to release the flavorful oils. *Serves 6*

1 whole chicken (about 4 pounds), cut into pieces (including back)

8 cups water

Coarse salt

2 medium onions, quartered

6 garlic cloves, smashed

½ cup coarsely chopped peeled fresh ginger, plus 3 thin slices

2 teaspoons canola or safflower oil

1¼ teaspoons whole coriander seeds

1 teaspoon whole cumin seeds

1 teaspoon whole mustard seeds (yellow or brown)

6 whole peeled tomatoes (from a 32-ounce can), finely chopped

1 serrano chile, thinly sliced

Scallion slices, for garnish

Orange halves, for serving

Bring chicken, the water, and 1 tablespoon salt to a boil in a stockpot, skimming off foam from surface with a large spoon. Add onions, garlic, and chopped ginger. Reduce heat and simmer, partially covered, 30 minutes.

Transfer chicken breast to a plate. Continue to simmer remaining chicken, partially covered, 30 minutes more. Transfer legs and thighs to plate. Let chicken cool slightly, then remove all meat from bones and slice.

Meanwhile, strain stock through a sieve and reserve; discard solids.

Heat oil in a stockpot over medium-high. Add spices and cook until fragrant and mustard seeds are popping, about 1 minute. Stir in tomatoes. Cook, stirring, until liquid has evaporated, about 4 minutes. Add reserved stock, the chile, and ginger slices. Simmer for 5 minutes, then skim off fat. Season with salt, and stir in sliced chicken. Garnish soup with scallions, squeeze orange halves over soup, and serve immediately.

DAIRY-FREE **NUT-FREE** GLUTEN-FREE

PER SERVING 583 CALORIES, 16 G FAT (4 G SATURATED FAT), 257 MG CHOLESTEROL, 9 G CARBOHYDRATES, 95 G PROTEIN, 2 G FIBER

225

quesadillas with collard greens and white beans

Quesadillas can be a vegetarian main course when given heft with greens and beans. The combination of collard greens and cannellini makes this filling particularly appealing. Corn tortillas can be used in place of whole-wheat ones for those avoiding gluten. *Serves 4*

2 tablespoons extra-virgin olive oil

1 shallot, thinly sliced

1 bunch collard greens (about 1½ pounds), stemmed, leaves chopped into ½-inch pieces

½ cup water

1½ cups cooked cannellini beans, drained and rinsed (see page 54)

Coarse salt and freshly ground pepper

8 whole-wheat tortillas (8-inch size)

2 cups grated sharp cheddar cheese

Fresh salsa, for serving

Heat oil in a large skillet over medium. Add shallot and sauté until tender, stirring occasionally, 2 to 4 minutes. Add collard greens and the water, stir to combine, and bring to a boil. Reduce heat, cover, and simmer until tender, about 10 minutes. Add beans, stir to combine, and cook until heated through. Season with salt and pepper.

Meanwhile, toast tortillas over the flame of a gas burner, turning, until lightly charred, about 1 minute (or char under the broiler).

Top each of 4 tortillas with ¼ cup cheese, then add collard greens, dividing evenly, and another ¼ cup cheese. Top with remaining tortillas. Toast in a large skillet until cheese is melted, about 6 minutes, flipping once. Serve with salsa.

NUT-FREE

PER SERVING 684 CALORIES, 31 G FAT (13 G
SATURATED FAT), 59 MG CHOLESTEROL, 76 G
CARBOHYDRATES, 30 G PROTEIN, 16 G FIBER

DAIRY-FREE **NUT-FREE** GLUTEN-FREE

PER SERVING 435 CALORIES, 19 G FAT (3 G SATURATED FAT), 125 MG CHOLESTEROL, 18 G CARBOHYDRATES, 47 G PROTEIN, 2 G FIBER

grilled chicken with cherry and arugula salad

Look beyond the dessert course for ways to use an abundance of peak-of-season fruits. Here, we've incorporated cherries into a protein-packed salad. If you don't have a cherry pitter, use a chef's knife: Gently press down on each cherry with the side of the blade, and remove the pit with your fingers. *Serves 2*

Canola or safflower oil, for grill

2 boneless, skinless chicken breast halves (4 to 5 ounces each)

2 tablespoons extra-virgin olive oil

Coarse salt and freshly ground pepper

1 teaspoon red-wine vinegar

1 small shallot, thinly sliced

8 ounces (2 cups) sweet cherries, pitted and halved

1 cup baby arugula

Heat grill (or grill pan) to medium-high; lightly oil hot grates.

Coat chicken with 1 tablespoon olive oil. Season with salt and pepper. Grill chicken until cooked through, 4 to 5 minutes per side. Transfer to a plate. Let stand for 5 minutes.

Meanwhile, whisk together remaining tablespoon olive oil, the vinegar, and shallot in a bowl. Add cherries and arugula, and toss to combine. Season with salt and pepper. Serve chicken topped with salad.

poached egg with rice and edamame

This ultra-delicious variation on the popular rice bowl is filled with good-for-you cleansing cabbage and kale, nutrient-rich brown rice, plus eggs and edamame for protein. *Serves 2*

1⅓ cups water

⅔ cup short-grain brown rice

Coarse salt

2 tablespoons extra-virgin olive oil

2 garlic cloves, sliced

⅛ teaspoon red-pepper flakes, plus more for serving

½ bunch kale, stemmed and chopped (4 cups)

1 cup (8 ounces) frozen shelled edamame, thawed

½ cup shredded red cabbage

2 large eggs

Bring the water, rice, and a pinch of salt to a boil in a saucepan. Reduce heat, cover, and simmer until grains are tender and water has been absorbed, 40 to 50 minutes. Remove from heat; let stand 10 minutes, then fluff with a fork.

Meanwhile, heat oil over medium in a large skillet. Add garlic and red-pepper flakes; cook until fragrant, about 30 seconds. Working in batches if necessary, add kale and cook, tossing, until wilted, about 2 minutes. Add edamame and cook, stirring, just until heated through. Season with salt. Transfer to a bowl with rice, and top with cabbage.

Bring 3 inches of water to a simmer in a skillet. Crack one egg at a time into a teacup or small bowl and gently slide into water. Cook until whites are just set and yolks are still loose, 3 to 4 minutes. Remove eggs from water using a slotted spoon.

To serve, divide rice and vegetables among bowls. Top each with an egg, and season with salt and red-pepper flakes.

DAIRY-FREE **NUT-FREE** GLUTEN-FREE

PER SERVING 615 CALORIES, 25 G FAT (4 G
SATURATED FAT), 212 MG CHOLESTEROL, 74 G
CARBOHYDRATES, 27 G PROTEIN, 11 G FIBER

poached chicken
with bok choy
in ginger broth

You'll want to make this veritable bowl of goodness anytime you feel a bit under the weather, to ward off a chill, or just because it is exceptionally satisfying. Regular bok choy can be used in place of baby bok choy; slice it into thin wedges. *Serves 4*

4½ cups chicken stock, preferably homemade (see recipe, page 314)

2 cups water

1 piece (1½ inches) fresh ginger, peeled and sliced

8 scallions, sliced (1 cup), plus more for garnish

2 Thai chiles or other hot chile peppers, 1 chopped (ribs and seeds removed for less heat, if desired), 1 sliced for garnish

1 cup dill sprigs

6 ounces shiitake mushrooms, caps sliced ¼ inch thick, stems reserved

2 whole boneless, skinless chicken breasts (10 to 12 ounces each)

2 heads baby bok choy, quartered into wedges

Combine stock, the water, ginger, scallions, chopped chile, the dill, and reserved mushroom stems in a pot over medium heat; bring to a boil, then reduce to a gentle simmer. Add chicken and poach until cooked through, 13 to 15 minutes.

Transfer chicken to a cutting board, and cover to keep warm. Strain stock through a fine sieve; discard solids. Return stock to pot, and bring to a simmer. Add mushroom caps and bok choy; simmer until tender, about 5 minutes.

To serve, slice chicken and divide among bowls, then ladle soup over chicken. Garnish with scallions and sliced chile.

DAIRY-FREE **NUT-FREE** GLUTEN-FREE

PER SERVING 191 CALORIES, 3 G FAT (1 G
SATURATED FAT), 41 MG CHOLESTEROL, 18 G
CARBOHYDRATES, 27 G PROTEIN, 7 G FIBER

seared halibut tacos with grapefruit-avocado salsa

The ever-popular fish taco need not rely on deep-fried strips to be delicious. Our tacos feature seared halibut and are served with a citrus salsa that would also make a great dip for slices of jicama. When searing the fillets, let them cook undisturbed until golden on the bottom before flipping, to get the crispest crust. *Serves 4*

1   Ruby Red grapefruit, segmented (see page 314) and cut into 1-inch pieces

1   avocado, halved, pitted, peeled, and sliced

2   tablespoons diced red onion

2   tablespoons chopped fresh cilantro leaves, plus sprigs for garnish

½   jalapeño chile, finely chopped (ribs and seeds removed for less heat, if desired)

1   tablespoon fresh lime juice

Coarse salt and freshly ground pepper

1   tablespoon extra-virgin olive oil

4   skinless halibut fillets (about 4 ounces each)

8   corn tortillas (6-inch size)

1   cup shredded napa cabbage

Combine grapefruit, avocado, red onion, cilantro, jalapeño, and lime juice in a bowl. Season with salt.

Heat oil in a large skillet over medium-high. Season halibut generously with salt and pepper. Cook until golden brown, 2 to 3 minutes. Flip and continue to cook until golden and flaky, 2 to 3 minutes more. Remove and let cool slightly, then flake with a fork.

Toast tortillas over the flame of a gas burner, turning, until lightly charred, about 1 minute. Top with fish, salsa, and cabbage, dividing evenly. Garnish with cilantro sprigs and serve immediately.

DAIRY-FREE **NUT-FREE** GLUTEN-FREE

PER SERVING 395 CALORIES, 15 G FAT
(2 G SATURATED FAT), 36 MG CHOLESTEROL,
38 G CARBOHYDRATES, 27 G PROTEIN, 6 G FIBER

VEGAN DAIRY-FREE **NUT-FREE** GLUTEN-FREE

PER SERVING 468 CALORIES, 26 G FAT (2 G SATURATED FAT), 0 MG CHOLESTEROL, 35 G CARBOHYDRATES, 26 G PROTEIN, 4 G FIBER

spinach, tofu, and brown rice bowl

Congee, or rice porridge, is the quintessential Chinese comfort food—and every home cook has her own variation. In this healthful version, brown rice is simmered with ginger and garlic and topped with tofu, baby spinach, and toasted sesame seeds. Kale or Swiss chard can replace the spinach; be sure to keep the ratio of greens to grains the same. *Serves 2*

6⅔ cups water

⅓ cup short-grain brown rice

Coarse salt and freshly ground pepper

½ package (14 ounces) firm tofu, drained, sliced into ¼-inch-thick pieces, and pressed (see page 314)

2 teaspoons tamari

1 tablespoon plus 1 teaspoon extra-virgin olive oil, plus more for baking sheet

1 tablespoon plus 1 teaspoon grated peeled fresh ginger

2 garlic cloves, minced

1 cup packed baby spinach

2 scallions, trimmed and thinly sliced

2 tablespoons sesame seeds, toasted (see page 314)

Bring ⅔ cup water, the rice, and a pinch of salt to a boil in a medium saucepan. Reduce heat, cover, and simmer until grains are tender and water has been absorbed, 40 to 50 minutes. Remove from heat; let stand 10 minutes, then fluff with a fork.

Preheat oven to 350°F. Place tofu in a bowl. Whisk together tamari and oil; season with salt and pepper. Drizzle dressing over tofu, and marinate 20 minutes, tossing occasionally.

Arrange tofu on an oiled baking sheet, and bake 10 minutes. Flip and bake 30 minutes more.

Meanwhile, fluff rice again with a fork, and add ginger, garlic, and remaining 6 cups water. Bring to a boil; cook, stirring occasionally, until broth has thickened, about 25 minutes. Season with salt. Serve immediately topped with tofu, spinach, scallions, and sesame seeds.

spicy cauliflower, bok choy, and shrimp stir-fry with coconut

This Southeast Asian stir-fry is an excellent way to eat more cruciferous vegetables (namely cauliflower and bok choy), among the best sources of the anti-inflammatory compounds known as glucosinolates. Try serving the dish over brown rice or other whole grains. *Serves 2*

1   tablespoon canola or safflower oil

¼   large head cauliflower, sliced ½ inch thick

½   large head bok choy, trimmed and sliced crosswise 1 inch thick

½   pound large shrimp, peeled and deveined

3   large garlic cloves, finely chopped

½   teaspoon sambal oelek or other hot chile sauce, or to taste

1   tablespoon honey

2   teaspoons fish sauce

½   cup fresh basil leaves, plus more for garnish

3   tablespoons unsweetened flaked coconut, toasted (see page 314)

Heat 1½ teaspoons oil in a wok or large cast-iron skillet over medium-high. Add cauliflower and reduce heat to medium. Cook, stirring occasionally, until golden brown, about 4 minutes. Add bok choy and cover. Cook, stirring occasionally, until vegetables are tender, about 8 minutes. Transfer vegetables to a plate, and cover to keep warm.

Heat 1 teaspoon oil in same skillet over medium-high. Add shrimp and cook until just opaque, about 2 minutes. Flip shrimp; using a wooden spoon, push to one side and add remaining ½ teaspoon oil. Add garlic and cook, stirring, until fragrant but not brown, about 1 minute.

Toss garlic with shrimp in skillet. Stir in sambal oelek, honey, and fish sauce. Add vegetables and cook until heated through, about 30 seconds. Stir in basil. Serve topped with coconut flakes and more basil.

DAIRY-FREE **NUT-FREE** GLUTEN-FREE

PER SERVING 298 CALORIES, 13 G FAT (4 G SATURATED FAT), 162 MG CHOLESTEROL, 14 G CARBOHYDRATES, 23 G PROTEIN, 5 G FIBER

DAIRY-FREE NUT-FREE

PER SERVING 568 CALORIES, 20 G FAT (3 G
SATURATED FAT), 60 MG CHOLESTEROL, 57 G
CARBOHYDRATES, 41 G PROTEIN, 13 G FIBER

black sea bass
with barley, shiitake,
and edamame salad

Black sea bass is prized for its tender but firm white flesh and sweet flavor. It's also versatile: Here, it's sautéed to a crisp, golden crust, but the fish is also excellent grilled, broiled, or roasted. The warm barley salad incorporates whole grains and legumes into the meal; try it also with chicken, or even on its own, for a satisfying lunch. *Serves 4*

2 cups water

1 cup pearl barley

Coarse salt and freshly ground pepper

¼ cup plus 1 tablespoon extra-virgin olive oil

8 ounces shiitake mushrooms, stemmed, sliced ¼ inch thick

3 shallots, minced

1 small garlic clove, minced

1½ cups frozen shelled edamame, thawed

4 skinless black sea bass fillets (about 4 ounces each)

2 limes, cut into wedges

Bring the water, barley, and a pinch of salt to a boil in a saucepan. Reduce heat, cover, and simmer until grains are tender and water has been absorbed, about 35 minutes. Remove from heat; let stand 10 minutes, then fluff with a fork.

Heat 3 tablespoons oil in a large skillet over medium-high. Add mushrooms; cook, stirring occasionally, until browned, about 8 minutes. Reduce heat to medium, and add shallots and garlic; cook until tender, about 3 minutes. Add edamame and cook, stirring occasionally, until heated through, about 3 minutes. Add barley and cook, stirring, until heated through, about 2 minutes. Season with salt and pepper. Transfer to a bowl, and cover to keep warm. Wipe pan clean.

Season fillets with salt and pepper. Heat remaining 2 tablespoons oil in pan over medium-high. Add fillets and cook until browned and crisp, about 3 minutes per side. Serve fillets atop barley salad, and squeeze lime wedges over fish.

lentil burgers with lettuce and yogurt

If you find yourself with leftover lentils, make these pan-seared patties—they're crisper, better tasting, and more healthful than store-bought (processed) vegetable burgers. Or start from scratch; the patties are worth the time. Serve them atop lettuce leaves, as here, or tucked into whole-wheat pita pockets. *Serves 4*

¾ cup French green lentils, picked over and rinsed

3 cups water

Coarse salt

1 small shallot, finely diced

2 large eggs, lightly whisked

1 cup plain fresh breadcrumbs

2 tablespoons chopped fresh flat-leaf parsley leaves, plus more for garnish

2 tablespoons extra-virgin olive oil, plus more for drizzling

1 head lettuce, such as escarole or Bibb, leaves separated

½ cup plain yogurt

Pinch of cayenne pepper

Caper berries and thinly sliced red onion, for serving

Bring lentils and the water to a boil in a small saucepan. Reduce to a simmer, season with salt, and cook until lentils are tender, about 20 minutes. Drain and let cool completely. (If not using immediately, let cool and refrigerate lentils in cooking liquid up to 1 week.)

Combine lentils, ½ teaspoon salt, the shallot, eggs, breadcrumbs, and parsley in a bowl. Pulse half of mixture in a food processor until smooth (or use a potato masher); fold remaining lentil into mixture.

Heat oil in a large skillet over medium-high. Scoop ¼ cup mixture, and shape into a 3-inch patty. Repeat with remaining mixture. Add to skillet, and cook until crisp and golden-brown, about 2 minutes per side. Transfer to a paper-towel-lined plate to drain. Let cool slightly.

To serve, top lettuce leaves with lentil patties. Season yogurt with salt, sprinkle with cayenne, and drizzle with oil. Garnish all with parsley. Serve with caper berries and red onion.

DAIRY-FREE **NUT-FREE** GLUTEN-FREE

PER SERVING 194 CALORIES, 4 G FAT (0 G
SATURATED FAT), 75 MG CHOLESTEROL, 8 G
CARBOHYDRATES, 34 G PROTEIN, 1 G FIBER

grilled chicken with cucumber, radish, and cherry tomato relish

Quick pickles (or relishes) add great flavor—without a lot of fat and calories—to lean proteins like fish or chicken. Homemade versions also contain much less sodium than those from a jar. Keep this simple pickling method in your back pocket for all sorts of vegetables, including wax beans, fennel, carrots, or zucchini. *Serves 6*

¼ cup white-wine vinegar, plus more for drizzling (optional)

¼ cup water

1 teaspoon turbinado sugar

2 garlic cloves, smashed

1 small jalapeño chile, quartered (ribs and seeds removed for less heat, if desired)

Coarse salt and freshly ground pepper

1 cucumber, peeled and diced

5 radishes, very thinly sliced

8 ounces cherry tomatoes, halved

1 small red onion, finely diced

Canola or safflower oil, for grill

6 boneless, skinless chicken breast halves (4 to 5 ounces each)

1 cup fresh mint leaves, torn, plus whole leaves for garnish

Combine vinegar, the water, sugar, garlic, jalapeño, and ¾ teaspoon salt in a small saucepan, and bring to a boil. Remove from heat, and let stand 15 minutes. Strain through a fine sieve; discard solids. Let cool completely.

Combine cucumber, radishes, tomatoes, and red onion in a bowl. Pour in vinegar mixture, and toss to coat.

Heat grill (or grill pan) to medium-high; lightly oil hot grates. Season chicken with salt and pepper. Working in batches, grill chicken until cooked through, 6 to 7 minutes per side. Transfer to a platter, and let stand 10 minutes. Stir torn mint into relish. Season with salt and pepper, and drizzle with vinegar, if desired. Spoon relish on top of chicken, and garnish with mint leaves.

caramelized fennel, celery, and sardine pasta

In this version of *pasta con le sarde,* a Sicilian classic, tinned sardines make a convenient (and just as healthful) replacement for fresh. Sardine bones, softened during canning, are barely noticeable—and full of calcium. Look for fennel with bright-green fronds attached, since they are essential to the dish. *Serves 4*

3 tablespoons extra-virgin olive oil, plus more for drizzling

1 large fennel bulb, trimmed, cored, and thinly sliced, plus ¼ cup chopped fennel fronds

2 celery stalks, thinly sliced on the bias, plus ¼ cup celery leaves

3 garlic cloves, thinly sliced

10 ounces whole-wheat penne rigate or other short tubular whole-wheat pasta

Coarse salt and freshly ground pepper

Grated zest of 1 lemon

1 tin (4.2 ounces) olive-oil-packed sardines, drained

Heat oil in a large skillet over medium-high. Add sliced fennel, sliced celery, and garlic; cook, stirring frequently, until tender and deep golden, about 8 minutes. Remove from heat.

Meanwhile, cook pasta in a pot of boiling salted water until al dente, according to package instructions. Reserve 1 cup pasta water; drain pasta.

Add pasta and reserved water to skillet with vegetables. Cook over medium-high heat, stirring to coat pasta, until warmed through, 2 to 3 minutes. Stir in fennel fronds, celery leaves, and lemon zest. Break up sardines into large pieces, and gently fold into pasta. Season with salt and pepper, drizzle with oil, and serve immediately.

DAIRY-FREE NUT-FREE

PER SERVING 406 CALORIES, 16 G FAT (2 G
SATURATED FAT), 48 MG CHOLESTEROL, 49 G
CARBOHYDRATES, 18 G PROTEIN, 11 G FIBER

VEGAN DAIRY-FREE **NUT-FREE** GLUTEN-FREE

PER SERVING 317 CALORIES, 15 G FAT (2 G
SATURATED FAT), 0 MG CHOLESTEROL, 44 G
CARBOHYDRATES, 5 G PROTEIN, 5 G FIBER

shiitake mushrooms and brown rice in parchment

Cooking en papillote is not only great for fish and chicken, it's also a nice option for vegetarian meals. The cooked brown rice gets "steamed" again in the packets, so it stays moist as it's infused with the flavors of mushrooms and thyme. It's one good reason to keep a batch of cooked brown rice on hand (the rice bowl on page 237 is another). *Serves 4*

1⅓ cups water

⅔ cup short-grain brown rice

Coarse salt and freshly ground pepper

10 ounces shiitake mushrooms, stemmed, thinly sliced (4 cups)

8 sprigs thyme

¼ cup extra-virgin olive oil

1 cup trimmed mixed greens, such as spinach, arugula, or watercress

Lemon wedges, for serving

Bring the water, rice, and a pinch of salt to a boil in a saucepan. Reduce heat, cover, and simmer until grains are tender and water has been absorbed, 40 to 50 minutes. Remove from heat; let stand 10 minutes, then fluff with a fork.

Preheat oven to 425°F. Cut four 12-by-17-inch pieces of parchment. Fold each in half crosswise to make a crease, then unfold and lay flat. Divide brown rice evenly among parchment pieces, creating a bed on one side of crease. Top with mushrooms and thyme. Season with salt and pepper, and drizzle with oil. Fold parchment over ingredients, creating a half-moon shape. Make small overlapping pleats to seal the open sides.

Bake on 2 rimmed baking sheets until packets are puffed, 20 to 25 minutes (mushrooms will be cooked through). Open packets; add greens, dividing evenly, and squeeze a lemon wedge over each one. Serve immediately.

wild salmon
with lentils and arugula

Besides being a classic pairing in French cooking, salmon and lentils are a dynamic duo of protein and other health-boosting nutrients. Neither one needs much in the way of flavor enhancers—just a fruity extra-virgin olive oil, fresh lemon juice, and the classic mirepoix of onion, carrot, and celery to start. *Serves 4*

1 red onion, diced

1 carrot, diced

1 celery stalk, diced

1 dried bay leaf

1 cup (8 ounces) green lentils, picked over and rinsed

Coarse salt and freshly ground pepper

2 tablespoons extra-virgin olive oil, plus more for drizzling

1 tablespoon fresh lemon juice, plus wedges for serving

3 cups baby arugula

4 skinless wild salmon fillets (about 5 ounces each)

Combine red onion, carrot, celery, bay leaf, and lentils in a pot. Add water to cover by 2 inches, and bring to a boil. Reduce to a simmer, and cook until lentils are tender, about 25 minutes. Drain, discarding bay leaf. Season with salt and pepper. Add oil and lemon juice. Stir in arugula, and cover to keep warm.

Meanwhile, preheat oven to 375°F. Arrange salmon in a baking dish. Drizzle with oil, and season with salt and pepper. Cover with parchment, then foil; bake until partially opaque in the middle, about 9 minutes. Serve salmon atop lentil salad, with lemon wedges.

DAIRY-FREE **NUT-FREE** GLUTEN-FREE

PER SERVING 439 CALORIES, 17 G FAT (2 G SATURATED FAT), 78 MG CHOLESTEROL, 32 G CARBOHYDRATES, 39 G PROTEIN, 8 G FIBER

mediterranean chicken stew
with COUSCOUS

All the health-promoting virtues of the Mediterranean diet are found in this stew: olive oil, leafy greens, tomatoes (in this case canned, which contain higher amounts of lycopene than raw ones), garlic, and chicken. Whole-wheat couscous provides more fiber and antioxidants than regular varieties; you could swap in a whole grain like farro in its place. *Serves 4*

1 tablespoon extra-virgin olive oil

3 boneless, skinless chicken breast halves (4 to 5 ounces each), cut into 1-inch pieces

Coarse salt and freshly ground pepper

1 onion, thinly sliced

4 garlic cloves, thinly sliced

½ teaspoon dried oregano

1 can (28 ounces) whole peeled tomatoes, in puree

⅓ cup water

⅓ cup whole-wheat couscous

1½ pounds escarole (about 2 medium heads), coarsely chopped

Heat oil in a Dutch oven or a large, heavy pot over medium-high. Season chicken with salt and pepper. Working in batches, cook chicken, tossing occasionally, until browned, about 5 minutes; transfer to a plate.

Add onion, garlic, and oregano to pot; season with salt and pepper. Cook, stirring occasionally, until onion begins to brown, 2 to 4 minutes. Add tomatoes (crushing with back of a spoon as you add them); cook until slightly thickened, 8 to 10 minutes.

Meanwhile, bring the water and a pinch of salt to a boil in a small saucepan. Stir in couscous, cover, and remove from heat. Let stand 5 minutes, then fluff with a fork. Cover to keep warm.

Add chicken with any accumulated juices to the pot, and bring to a simmer; cover and cook until chicken is cooked through, 2 to 4 minutes. Add as much escarole to pot as will fit. Cook, tossing and adding more as space becomes available. Cook until escarole is tender, 2 to 4 minutes. Serve stew over couscous.

DAIRY-FREE **NUT-FREE**

PER SERVING 295 CALORIES, 7 G FAT (2 G
SATURATED FAT), 65 MG CHOLESTEROL, 26 G
CARBOHYDRATES, 30 G PROTEIN, 11 G FIBER

buttermilk-poached chicken with escarole and radicchio

Buttermilk creates a tenderizing poaching liquid for boneless, skinless chicken breasts, yielding a luxuriant texture. More buttermilk (and yogurt) goes into the dressing served alongside. Watermelon radishes are shown here, but any type of radish will work just fine. *Serves 6*

6   boneless, skinless chicken breasts (4 to 5 ounces each)

1   quart buttermilk

4   sprigs sage

4   garlic cloves, smashed

    Coarse salt and freshly ground pepper

1   cup plain Greek yogurt

1   small shallot, minced

¼   cup finely chopped cornichons

2   teaspoons capers, rinsed and drained

1   teaspoon finely grated lemon zest, plus 1 tablespoon fresh juice

1   small head escarole, leaves torn

1   small head radicchio, leaves separated

4   radishes, thinly sliced

¼   cup sliced almonds, toasted (see page 314)

Let chicken stand at room temperature 30 minutes. Reserve 3 tablespoons buttermilk for dressing; place remaining buttermilk, the sage, and garlic in a Dutch oven or a large, heavy pot. Season chicken with salt and pepper, and submerge in buttermilk mixture in a single layer.

Heat mixture over medium, stirring occasionally, until just shimmering (do not let buttermilk simmer, or it will curdle). Poach chicken, turning pieces occasionally, until cooked through, about 15 minutes; adjust heat as necessary to keep liquid from reaching a simmer. Transfer chicken to a dish and let cool. Discard poaching liquid.

In a bowl, combine yogurt, shallot, cornichons, capers, lemon zest and juice, and reserved buttermilk. Season with salt. Arrange escarole and radicchio on a platter. Top with chicken, radishes, and almonds. Serve dressing on the side.

VEGAN DAIRY-FREE

PER SERVING 608 CALORIES, 37 G FAT (5 G
SATURATED FAT), 0 MG CHOLESTEROL, 62 G
CARBOHYDRATES, 13 G PROTEIN, 12 G FIBER

farro spaghetti with fresh tomatoes and marcona almonds

Little more than fresh, ripe, juicy tomatoes make up this no-cook pasta sauce. Marinating the tomatoes for at least one hour (and up to three) allows them to soak up all the other flavors, which pair nicely with the whole-grain noodles. Chopped Marcona almonds replace breadcrumbs for a crunchy component. *Serves 4*

3 large tomatoes (about 2 pounds), cored and coarsely chopped

½ cup extra-virgin olive oil

2 garlic cloves, thinly sliced

½ teaspoon red-pepper flakes

½ cup fresh basil leaves, plus more for garnish

Coarse salt

10 ounces farro spaghetti

⅓ cup chopped Marcona almonds, for garnish

Combine tomatoes, oil, garlic, red-pepper flakes, basil, and a pinch of salt in a bowl; let stand 1 to 3 hours at room temperature.

Meanwhile, cook spaghetti in a pot of boiling salted water until al dente, according to package instructions. Drain and return pasta to pot. Add tomato sauce and toss to combine.

Garnish each serving with almonds and basil before serving.

almond-crusted chicken breast
with spinach

Nuts offer a gluten-free way to make "breaded" chicken cutlets that are as crisp and tasty as the original (some say, even better). Here, toasted almonds are ground to a paste with garlic and extra-virgin olive oil, then patted over the chicken breasts before roasting. *Serves 2*

½ cup almonds, toasted (see page 314)

3 tablespoons extra-virgin olive oil

1 garlic clove

Coarse salt and freshly ground pepper

2 boneless, skinless chicken breast halves (4 to 5 ounces each)

3 ounces baby spinach

Lemon wedges, for serving

Preheat oven to 425°F. Pulse almonds, oil, garlic, and ½ teaspoon salt to a coarse paste in a food processor. Season chicken with salt and pepper. Rub almond paste over chicken, dividing evenly.

Roast chicken on a rimmed baking sheet until cooked through, 15 to 18 minutes. Transfer to a cutting board and slice. Serve chicken over baby spinach with lemon wedges.

DAIRY-FREE GLUTEN-FREE

PER SERVING 373 CALORIES, 21 G FAT (2 G
SATURATED FAT), 82 MG CHOLESTEROL, 9 G
CARBOHYDRATES, 41 G PROTEIN, 6 G FIBER

black cod with herbs, zucchini, and whole-wheat couscous

Also known as sablefish, black cod—which is not related to codfish—rivals wild salmon in omega-3 fatty acid content. It has a mild buttery flavor and firm white flesh similar to cod and halibut (either of which can be used in its place). You could also serve the dish with quinoa or brown rice instead of whole-wheat couscous. *Serves 4*

6 scallions, trimmed and chopped

1 cup packed fresh cilantro leaves

½ cup packed fresh mint leaves

3 tablespoons extra-virgin olive oil

1 tablespoon finely chopped peeled fresh ginger

¾ teaspoon ground coriander (optional)

Coarse salt and freshly ground pepper

1 zucchini, cut lengthwise into ¾-inch-thick spears

4 skinless black cod fillets (about 5 ounces each)

⅓ cup water

⅓ cup whole-wheat couscous

Preheat oven to 425°F. Pulse scallions, cilantro, mint, oil, ginger, coriander, and ½ teaspoon salt in a food processor until a coarse paste forms. Season with pepper.

Toss zucchini with 3 tablespoons herb paste in a bowl. Arrange in a single layer on a rimmed baking sheet. Roast for 5 minutes. Remove from oven.

Rub remaining herb paste onto both sides of fish fillets. Push zucchini to edges of baking sheet, and arrange fish in center, leaving about ½ inch between each fillet. Roast until fish is opaque and semifirm to the touch, about 15 minutes.

Meanwhile, bring the water and a pinch of salt to a boil in a small saucepan. Stir in couscous, cover, and remove from heat. Let stand 5 minutes, then fluff with a fork.

Serve fish over couscous with zucchini on the side.

DAIRY-FREE NUT-FREE

PER SERVING 323 CALORIES, 12 G FAT (2 G
SATURATED FAT), 78 MG CHOLESTEROL, 16 G
CARBOHYDRATES, 37 G PROTEIN, 5 G FIBER

sautéed mushrooms with toasted flatbread and baked eggs

Hearty one-pot vegetarian meals like this one are a boon to the home cook, since they are equally welcome at the family dinner table or when welcoming friends for brunch. A mixture of different mushrooms produces the best results; vary the amount of red-pepper flakes to suit your preference. *Serves 4*

1 whole-wheat flatbread (6-inch size)

3 tablespoons extra-virgin olive oil

2 garlic cloves, thinly sliced

1 pound mixed mushrooms, such as cremini, shiitake, and oyster, trimmed and thinly sliced

Coarse salt

Red-pepper flakes

¼ cup dry white wine

2 tablespoons fresh thyme leaves

4 large eggs, room temperature

Preheat oven to 425°F. Toast flatbread over the flame of a gas burner (or char under the broiler). Tear into 2-inch pieces.

Heat oil in a large ovenproof skillet over medium. Add garlic and cook until fragrant but not browned, about 1 minute. Increase heat to medium-high and add mushrooms. Cook, stirring occasionally, until tender and golden brown, about 10 minutes. Season with salt and red-pepper flakes. Add wine and deglaze, scraping up browned bits from the bottom of the pan. Stir in flatbread pieces and thyme, and remove skillet from heat.

Make 4 shallow wells in the mushroom mixture and crack 1 egg into each well. Transfer to the oven, and cook until whites are just set and yolks are still loose, about 4 minutes. Season eggs with salt and red-pepper flakes. Serve immediately.

DAIRY-FREE NUT-FREE

PER SERVING 256 CALORIES, 16 G FAT (3 G
SATURATED FAT), 212 MG CHOLESTEROL, 17 G
CARBOHYDRATES, 11 G PROTEIN, 2 G FIBER

DAIRY-FREE **NUT-FREE** GLUTEN-FREE

PER SERVING 229 CALORIES, 15 G FAT (2 G
SATURATED FAT), 39 MG CHOLESTEROL, 10 G
CARBOHYDRATES, 16 G PROTEIN, 4 G FIBER

grapefruit, salmon, and avocado salad

Naturally detoxifying grapefruit and heart-healthy avocado join forces with omega-3-rich salmon in this winter salad. Baked salmon calls for little added fat (here, extra-virgin olive oil) to be moist and achieve just the right texture for breaking into pieces. *Serves 4*

2   skinless wild salmon fillets (about 5 ounces each)

Coarse salt and freshly ground pepper

1   tablespoon extra-virgin olive oil, plus more for serving

2   scallions, trimmed and thinly sliced

1   Ruby Red grapefruit, segmented (see page 314)

1   avocado, halved, pitted, peeled, and sliced

2   cups trimmed mixed tender greens, such as watercress and sunflower shoots

Lime wedges, for drizzling

Preheat oven to 375°F. Season salmon with salt and pepper, and arrange in a baking dish. Drizzle with oil, then sprinkle with 1 sliced scallion. Bake until partially opaque in the middle, about 10 minutes. Let cool slightly, and break up fish into large pieces.

Arrange salmon on a platter, and top with remaining scallion, the grapefruit, avocado, and greens. Drizzle with oil, and squeeze lime wedges over salad. Season with salt and pepper and serve immediately.

red lentil soup with turnip and parsley

If you're more familiar with brown or green varieties, consider adding red lentils to your pantry. Here, they are paired with turnip in a super-simple soup. Turnips are slightly sweet and peppery, and a very good source of vitamin C. Peel and shred them (like carrots) for slaws or salads; or toss with olive oil and herbs, and roast them in the oven. *Serves 8*

2 tablespoons olive oil

1 yellow onion, diced

4 garlic cloves, minced

3 celery stalks, finely diced

3 tomatoes, chopped

1½ cups dried red lentils, picked over and rinsed

1 turnip, peeled and diced

6 cups water

½ cup chopped fresh flat-leaf parsley leaves, plus more for garnish

1 teaspoon red-wine vinegar

Coarse salt and freshly ground pepper

Heat oil in a pot over medium. Add onion, garlic, and celery; cook, stirring occasionally, until tender, 6 to 8 minutes.

Increase heat to high, and add tomatoes; cook, stirring, 1 minute. Stir in lentils, turnip, and the water, and bring to a boil. Reduce heat and simmer until lentils are tender, 20 to 25 minutes. Stir in parsley and vinegar. Season with salt and pepper. Serve soup immediately, garnished with additional parsley.

VEGAN DAIRY-FREE NUT-FREE GLUTEN-FREE

PER SERVING 190 CALORIES, 5 G FAT (1 G SATURATED FAT), 0 MG CHOLESTEROL, 28 G CARBOHYDRATES, 11 G PROTEIN, 7 G FIBER

PER SERVING 605 CALORIES, 29 G FAT (7 G
SATURATED FAT), 6 MG CHOLESTEROL, 73 G
CARBOHYDRATES, 21 G PROTEIN, 15 G FIBER

spaghetti with collard greens and lemon

This wholesome pasta dish strikes just the right balance of greens and noodles, with ample flavor provided by lots of lemon (zest and juice) and some finely grated sharp cheese. Pine nuts are a good source of heart-healthy fats; choose nuts from the United States, Europe, or Turkey (these will be long and thin) over those from China (short and round). *Serves 4*

2 tablespoons extra-virgin olive oil

2 garlic cloves, sliced

¼ teaspoon red-pepper flakes

1 bunch collard greens (12 ounces), ribs removed, thinly sliced

¼ cup pine nuts, toasted (see page 314)

Grated zest of 1 lemon, plus more for garnish

2 tablespoons fresh lemon juice

Coarse salt

12 ounces whole-grain spaghetti, such as farro

¼ cup finely grated Pecorino Romano cheese

Heat oil in a large skillet over medium. Add garlic and red-pepper flakes; cook until tender, about 1 minute. Add collard greens and cook, stirring, until tender, about 5 minutes. Remove from heat, and stir in pine nuts and lemon zest and juice. Season with salt.

Meanwhile, cook spaghetti in a pot of salted boiling water until al dente, according to package instructions. Reserve 1 cup pasta water; drain pasta.

Add pasta and reserved water to skillet, tossing to coat. Serve immediately, garnished with lemon zest and sprinkled with cheese.

trout, tomatoes, and basil in parchment

The best time to make these lovely packets is during the summer, when basil and tomatoes are at their most flavorful. A mere drizzle of extra-virgin olive oil over the fish before sealing the parchment is sufficient to aid in steaming during cooking. Serve as is, or over brown rice or other whole grain. *Serves 4*

4   skinless rainbow trout fillets (about 5 ounces each), bones removed

Coarse salt and freshly ground pepper

2   small tomatoes, thinly sliced

Extra-virgin olive oil, for drizzling

1   cup fresh basil leaves

Preheat oven to 400°F. Cut four 12-by-17-inch pieces of parchment. Fold each in half crosswise to make a crease, then unfold and lay flat. Arrange each fillet in the center of a parchment rectangle. Season with salt and pepper, and top with tomatoes. Drizzle with oil. Fold parchment over ingredients, creating a half-moon shape. Make small overlapping pleats to seal the open sides.

Bake on 2 rimmed baking sheets until packets are puffed, 12 to 14 minutes (fish will be opaque through-out). Serve immediately, cutting open packets and garnishing fish with basil at the table.

DAIRY-FREE **NUT-FREE** GLUTEN-FREE

PER SERVING 230 CALORIES, 9 G FAT (2 G
SATURATED FAT), 94 MG CHOLESTEROL, 2 G
CARBOHYDRATES, 33 G PROTEIN, 1 G FIBER

DAIRY-FREE **NUT-FREE** GLUTEN-FREE

PER SERVING 741 CALORIES, 21 G FAT (5 G
SATURATED FAT), 108 MG CHOLESTEROL, 71 G
CARBOHYDRATES, 60 G PROTEIN, 19 G FIBER

spicy north african chicken-chickpea stew

Chicken and chickpeas give this dish plenty of protein; cinnamon, cumin, ginger, garlic, cilantro, and lemon (peel and all) make it incredibly flavorful and wonderfully cleansing. Follow the stew with Pistachio-Stuffed Dates (see recipe, page 296) and fresh mint tea for a North African–inspired meal. *Serves 4*

1 tablespoon extra-virgin olive oil

3 onions, thinly sliced

1 tablespoon minced peeled fresh ginger

3 garlic cloves, thinly sliced

½ teaspoon ground cumin

3½ cups cooked chickpeas (see page 54), drained and rinsed

4 plum tomatoes, coarsely chopped

½ small lemon, seeded and finely chopped (including peel), plus wedges for serving

3 sticks cinnamon

1 whole chicken (about 4 pounds), cut into 10 pieces, skin removed

Coarse salt and freshly ground pepper

1½ cups water

¼ cup coarsely chopped cilantro, plus more for garnish

Heat oil in a stockpot over medium. Add onions, ginger, and garlic; cook, stirring frequently, until onions are soft and translucent, about 10 minutes. Add cumin and cook, stirring, for 30 seconds. Add chickpeas, tomatoes, chopped lemon, and cinnamon sticks; cook, stirring, until tomatoes soften slightly, about 3 minutes.

Season chicken with salt and pepper; add to pot. Add the water, nestling chicken into liquid. Bring to a boil. Reduce to a gentle simmer, and cook, partially covered, until chicken is cooked through, about 40 minutes. Remove chicken.

Increase heat to high, and continue cooking to reduce liquid slightly, if necessary, crushing some chickpeas to thicken. Stir in cilantro. Season with more salt and pepper. Spoon chickpeas and liquid into bowls, and top with chicken. Garnish with additional cilantro, and serve immediately with lemon wedges.

shrimp, cod, and fennel soup with tomatoes

This take on bouillabaisse features shrimp and cod, both lean proteins and good sources of omega-3 fatty acids, in a base of fish stock bulked up with tomatoes and fennel. Contrary to their reputation as a high-cholesterol food, shrimp have been shown to raise good cholesterol levels and lower triglyceride levels (another risk factor for heart disease). *Serves 4*

2 vine-ripened tomatoes

2 tablespoons extra-virgin olive oil

1 small onion, finely chopped

2 garlic cloves, minced

1 small bulb fennel, quartered lengthwise, cored, thinly sliced crosswise, fronds reserved for garnish

Coarse salt and freshly ground white pepper

1 cup dry white wine or water

4 cups fish stock, preferably home-made (see recipe, page 315)

12 ounces skinless cod fillets, cut into 1½-inch pieces

¾ pound medium shrimp, peeled and deveined (tails left intact)

Score an X in the bottom of each tomato using a sharp paring knife. Blanch tomatoes in a pot of boiling water until skins loosen, 30 seconds to 1 minute. Transfer to an ice-water bath using a slotted spoon and let cool. Peel and discard skins. Core and coarsely chop tomatoes.

Heat 1 tablespoon oil in a Dutch oven or a large, heavy pot over medium-high. Add onion, garlic, and sliced fennel; cook until softened, stirring occasionally, 3 to 5 minutes. Season with salt and white pepper. Add wine. Return to heat; bring to a boil, scraping up brown bits from bottom of pot. Cook until reduced by half, about 2 minutes.

Add stock and tomatoes; bring to a simmer. Stir in cod and shrimp, and return to a simmer. Remove from heat; let stand, stirring halfway through, until cod and shrimp are just cooked through, about 3 minutes.

Serve soup drizzled with remaining tablespoon oil and garnished with fennel fronds.

DAIRY-FREE **NUT-FREE** GLUTEN-FREE

PER SERVING 374 CALORIES, 10 G FAT (2 G
SATURATED FAT), 169 MG CHOLESTEROL, 14 G
CARBOHYDRATES, 43 G PROTEIN, 3 G FIBER

grilled salmon
and bok choy with
orange-avocado salsa

Invoke tropical climes with this sunny salsa, a mix of orange and avocado with just a touch of toasted sesame oil. If grilling is not an option, use a grill pan or the broiler to cook the salmon and bok choy. *Serves 2*

Canola or safflower oil, for grill

1 navel orange, segmented (see page 314)

½ avocado, peeled and diced

1 tablespoon chopped red onion

1 tablespoon chopped fresh cilantro leaves

1 teaspoon fresh lime juice

¼ teaspoon toasted sesame oil

Coarse salt and freshly ground pepper

2 skinless wild salmon fillets (about 5 ounces each)

3 heads bok choy, halved lengthwise

Extra-virgin olive oil, for drizzling

Heat grill (or grill pan) to medium-high; lightly oil hot grates. In a bowl, combine orange, avocado, red onion, cilantro, lime juice, and sesame oil. Season with salt and pepper.

Season salmon and bok choy with salt and pepper, and drizzle with oil. Grill salmon, flipping halfway through, until partially opaque in the center, 3 to 4 minutes per side. Grill bok choy until bright green and slightly wilted, about 1 minute per side.

Spoon avocado salsa over fish. Serve immediately, with bok choy on the side.

DAIRY-FREE NUT-FREE GLUTEN-FREE

spinach tart with olive-oil cracker crust

More greens, less crust is what makes this take on spanakopita so much better for you. Plus, there's no butter in the crust and less cheese in the filling. The tart is easy enough for a weeknight dinner, but worth keeping in mind for vegetarian guests during the holidays. *Serves 6*

¾ cup whole-wheat flour

¾ cup spelt flour

2 tablespoons plus ½ teaspoon sesame seeds

1½ teaspoons coarse salt

⅓ cup plus 1 tablespoon extra-virgin olive oil

⅓ cup water

1½ pounds spinach, stemmed (about 14 packed cups)

1 large shallot, finely chopped

1 garlic clove, minced

¼ teaspoon red-pepper flakes, plus more for garnish

⅓ cup feta cheese, crumbled (about 2 ounces)

2 large eggs, lightly beaten

Preheat oven to 425°F. Whisk together both flours, 2 tablespoons sesame seeds, and 1 teaspoon salt in a bowl. Stir in ⅓ cup oil and the water; knead until a ball forms. Roll out dough into a 12-inch round. Fit into a 9½-inch tart pan with a removable bottom; trim any excess. Prick bottom all over with a fork. Bake until golden brown, about 35 minutes. Let cool on a wire rack.

Reduce oven temperature to 350°F. Rinse spinach and place in a large pot, with water clinging to leaves. Cover; cook over medium, tossing occasionally, until just wilted, about 6 minutes. Transfer to a colander to drain. Squeeze spinach in a kitchen towel to remove excess water. Coarsely chop and transfer to a bowl.

Wipe pot clean. Heat remaining tablespoon oil over medium. Cook shallot, garlic, and red-pepper flakes, stirring, until softened, about 4 minutes. Transfer to bowl with spinach. Stir in feta, eggs, and remaining ½ teaspoon salt. Pour into crust; sprinkle with remaining ½ teaspoon sesame seeds. Bake until filling is just set, 30 to 35 minutes. Serve garnished with red-pepper flakes.

NUT-FREE

PER SERVING 317 CALORIES, 20 G FAT (4 G SATURATED FAT), 78 MG CHOLESTEROL, 26 G CARBOHYDRATES, 11 G PROTEIN, 6 G FIBER

watercress, sardine,
and orange salad

Heart-healthy sardines from a tin make this salad a convenient option for weeknight meals. Watercress, clementines, and toasted pumpkin seeds contribute loads of nutrients along with appealing flavors, textures, and colors. *Serves 2*

2 clementines

Grated zest and juice of ½ lemon

1 tablespoon extra-virgin olive oil

Coarse salt and freshly ground pepper

2 cups trimmed watercress, such as Upland cress

¼ small red onion, sliced

1 tablespoon fresh tarragon leaves

1 tin (4.2 ounces) olive-oil-packed sardines, drained

3 tablespoons raw hulled pumpkin seeds (pepitas), toasted (see page 314)

Use a paring knife to cut peel and pith away from clementines, following curve of the fruit. Slice clementines into rounds, and remove any seeds.

Whisk together lemon zest and juice with oil in a bowl, and season with salt and pepper.

Arrange watercress, red onion, and tarragon on a platter. Top with clementines, sardines, and pumpkin seeds. Season with salt and pepper. Drizzle with vinaigrette and serve immediately.

DAIRY-FREE **NUT-FREE** GLUTEN-FREE

PER SERVING 281 CALORIES, 16 G FAT (3 G SATURATED FAT), 85 MG CHOLESTEROL, 14 G CARBOHYDRATES, 23 G PROTEIN, 2 G FIBER

DAIRY-FREE **NUT-FREE** GLUTEN-FREE

PER SERVING 287 CALORIES, 11 G FAT (2 G
SATURATED FAT), 80 MG CHOLESTEROL, 11 G
CARBOHYDRATES, 35 G PROTEIN, 3 G FIBER

poached salmon with fennel and grapefruit

Poaching gives salmon a wonderfully silken texture and infuses it with the subtle flavor of the aromatics it is cooked with, which mellow and soften. Here, grapefruit (zest and juice) is a nice alternative to the usual lemon. Rustic bread is just right for sopping up the cooking liquid, which doubles as a broth for serving, if desired. *Serves 4*

1 Ruby Red grapefruit

4 cups fish stock, preferably homemade (see recipe, page 315)

1 small red onion, sliced into wedges, root end attached

1 small fennel bulb, sliced lengthwise, root end attached, plus 2 stalks with fronds

10 whole black peppercorns

4 cups water

Coarse salt

4 skinless wild salmon fillets (about 5 ounces each)

Use a vegetable peeler to remove the grapefruit zest in long strips, then squeeze ¼ cup juice. Transfer to a Dutch oven or a large, heavy pot. Add stock, red onion, fennel, peppercorns, and the water; season with salt. Bring to a gentle simmer, cover, and cook until the fennel is tender, about 10 minutes.

Submerge fish in cooking liquid; cook at a steady simmer until salmon is cooked through, about 5 minutes. Transfer fillets to plates and serve with fennel, onion, and zest.

ginger-scallion chicken breasts in parchment

Boneless, skinless chicken breasts cook quickly and pair well with a range of spices and seasonings, including the Asian ones here. Reserve the mushroom soaking liquid for making vegetable stock or risotto. *Serves 4*

5 ounces (about ⅓ cup) dried shiitake mushrooms

1 cup boiling water

¼ cup tamari

½ teaspoon toasted sesame oil

¼ cup rice vinegar

2 teaspoons honey

1 piece (4 inches) peeled fresh ginger: 3 inches finely grated; the remainder sliced

4 scallions, white and light-green parts only, finely chopped; plus more, julienned, for garnish

2 whole boneless, skinless chicken breasts (10 to 12 ounces each)

Preheat oven to 400°F. Soak mushrooms in the boiling water until soft, about 15 minutes. Lift mushrooms with a slotted spoon or a sieve; thinly slice mushrooms.

Stir together tamari, sesame oil, vinegar, honey, and sliced ginger in a baking dish. Stir together chopped scallions and grated ginger in a bowl.

Cut chicken in half lengthwise to make 4 pieces total. Make a slit in one side of each piece to create a pocket, leaving other side intact. Spoon scallion-ginger mixture into each piece, dividing evenly. Transfer chicken to baking dish with tamari mixture. Marinate at room temperature, turning halfway through, 20 minutes.

Cut four 12-by-17-inch pieces of parchment. Fold each in half crosswise to make a crease, then unfold and lay flat. Arrange a chicken piece on one side of crease of each parchment rectangle; top with mushrooms. Fold parchment over ingredients, creating a half-moon shape. Make small overlapping pleats to seal open sides. Cook on 2 rimmed baking sheets 10 minutes (chicken will be cooked through). Open packets, garnish with julienned scallions, and serve immediately.

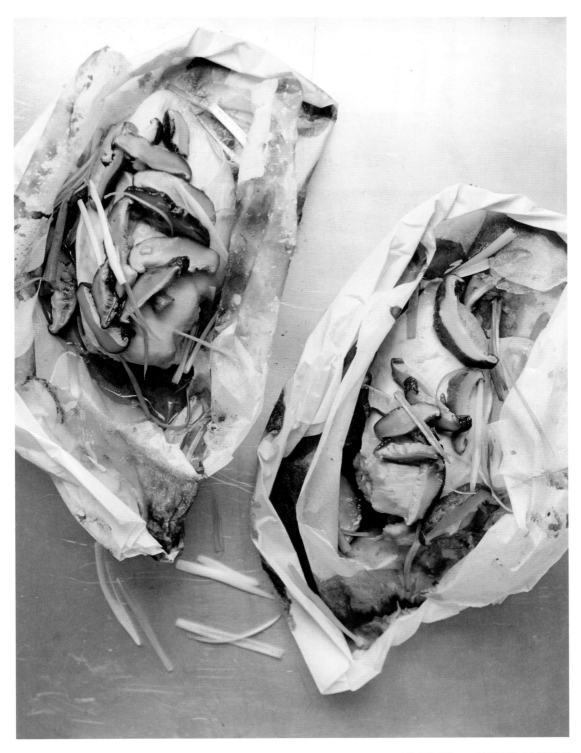

DAIRY-FREE **NUT-FREE** GLUTEN-FREE

brown rice with salmon, avocado, and toasted nori

Skip the takeout sushi and prepare a Japanese-inspired dinner from scratch instead. Serve extra toasted nori sheets on their own for an excellent protein- and nutrient-rich snack. *Serves 4*

2½ cups water

1¼ cups short-grain brown rice

Coarse salt

1 teaspoon canola oil

4 pieces sushi-grade salmon (each about 4 ounces and 1 inch thick)

2 sheets nori

3 tablespoons fresh lemon juice

3 tablespoons reduced-sodium soy sauce

1½ teaspoons hot chile sauce

1 avocado, halved, pitted, peeled, and sliced

1 English cucumber, halved lengthwise and thinly sliced on the bias

¼ cup cilantro sprigs

1 small Thai chile, thinly sliced, for garnish (optional)

Bring the water, rice, and a pinch of salt to a boil in a saucepan. Reduce heat, cover, and simmer until grains are tender and water has been absorbed, 40 to 50 minutes. Remove from heat; let stand 10 minutes, then fluff with a fork.

Heat oil in a nonstick pan over high. Pat fish dry. Cook fish until golden-brown on outside but still rare in center, 1½ to 2 minutes per side. Let cool slightly.

Meanwhile, using tongs, toast nori sheets, one at a time, over the flame of a gas burner until they begin to shrivel and are fragrant.

Mix together lemon juice, soy sauce, and chile sauce in a bowl. Divide rice among 4 plates, and drizzle with half the sauce. Arrange avocado and cucumber on top of rice. Break salmon into chunks, and divide among plates. Drizzle with remaining sauce, and top with cilantro and chile, if desired. Break nori into pieces, and serve on the side.

DAIRY-FREE **NUT-FREE** GLUTEN-FREE

almond chicken soup
with sweet potato, collards, and ginger

A full two tablespoons of minced fresh ginger provides this soup—inspired by classic North African nut stews—with significant warming properties as well as ample antioxidants. Collards, sweet potato, and almond butter (to thicken the broth) up the nutritional ante. *Serves 4*

4 cups chicken stock, preferably homemade (see recipe, page 314)

½ yellow onion, finely chopped

1 garlic clove, minced

1 large sweet potato, peeled and finely chopped

8 ounces boneless, skinless chicken breast, cut into 1-inch pieces

½ cup smooth almond butter (see recipe, page 315)

1 cup chopped trimmed collard green leaves

2 tablespoons minced peeled fresh ginger

Coarse salt and freshly ground pepper

Lime wedges, for serving

Combine stock, onion, garlic, and sweet potato in a stockpot, and bring to a boil. Reduce to a simmer, and add the chicken; cover and simmer 20 minutes.

In a bowl, whisk together almond butter and ½ cup of hot broth into a thick paste.

Add collard leaves and ginger to soup; bring to a boil, then reduce the heat and simmer, covered, 5 minutes. Stir in almond-butter paste. Season with salt and pepper. Serve soup immediately with lime wedges.

DAIRY-FREE GLUTEN-FREE

PER SERVING 348 CALORIES, 21 G FAT (3 G SATURATED FAT), 48 MG CHOLESTEROL, 17 G CARBOHYDRATES, 26 G PROTEIN, 3 G FIBER

moroccan-steamed salmon with quinoa and carrots

Cilantro, a powerful antioxidant, is processed with garlic, lemon, olive oil, cumin, and red-pepper flakes to make a versatile sauce. This time it's served with salmon, but it will also pair nicely with other types of fish, such as rainbow trout or halibut, as well as chicken; or drizzle over roasted vegetables or grain-based salads. *Serves 2*

1 cup water

½ cup quinoa, rinsed and drained

1 carrot, finely chopped

Coarse salt

2 cups fresh cilantro leaves, plus more for garnish

1 garlic clove, crushed

3 tablespoons extra-virgin olive oil, plus more for brushing

2 tablespoons fresh lemon juice

½ teaspoon cumin powder

¼ teaspoon red-pepper flakes

2 skinless wild salmon fillets (about 5 ounces each)

Bring the water, quinoa, carrot, and ¼ teaspoon salt to a boil in a small saucepan. Reduce heat, cover, and simmer until liquid has been absorbed and quinoa is tender but still chewy, about 15 minutes. Transfer to a large bowl, then fluff with a fork.

Pulse cilantro, garlic, oil, lemon juice, cumin, and red-pepper flakes in a food processor until smooth. Season with salt.

Lightly season salmon with salt. Brush bottom of a metal steamer basket (or colander) with oil. (If using a bamboo steamer, line bottom with a large lettuce leaf or a parchment round.) Arrange salmon in steamer, and set over boiling water; steam, covered, until partially opaque in the middle, 6 to 9 minutes.

Serve salmon over couscous; top with cilantro sauce, and garnish with additional cilantro.

DAIRY-FREE **NUT-FREE** GLUTEN-FREE

PER SERVING 577 CALORIES, 33 G FAT (5 G SATURATED FAT), 78 MG CHOLESTEROL, 35 G CARBOHYDRATES, 35 G PROTEIN, 4 G FIBER

relax

---

have a little something sweet

Taking a moment for pure enjoyment is an equally important part of a whole-foods diet. Think of it as nurturing mind, body, and soul. You'll find plenty of delicious options for fruit and chocolate (and more) that just happen to be wholesome as well.

fruit While fruit is certainly the most obvious "clean slate" dessert, serving it on its own can feel less than exciting. All it takes is an inspired approach—and a bit of unexpected texture or another flavor note—for fruit to go from simple to extra-special.

citrus salad with
pomegranate

pistachio-
stuffed dates
with coconut

roasted plums
with **yogurt**
and **granola**

no-bake oat bars
with **strawberries**

pistachio-stuffed dates with coconut

16 dates, pitted
½ cup unsalted shelled pistachios
   Pinch of coarse salt
1 tablespoon unsweetened shredded coconut, toasted (see page 314)

Use a paring knife to split open dates, leaving other side intact. Puree pistachios in a food processor until a thick paste forms, about 5 minutes. Season with salt. Spoon mixture into dates. Top with coconut. *Makes 16*

citrus salad with pomegranate

4 pounds mixed citrus such as navel, Cara Cara, mandarin, and blood oranges; grapefruit; and Meyer lemons
½ cup pomegranate seeds (from ½ large pomegranate)

Use a paring knife to cut away peel and pith of citrus, following the curve of the fruit. Slice some fruit into rounds, and separate others into segments (see page 314).

Arrange citrus on a platter, and sprinkle with pomegranate seeds before serving. *Serves 4*

no-bake oat bars with strawberries

1½ cups pitted dates
¼   cup raw macadamia nuts
2   tablespoons old-fashioned rolled oats
     Pinch of sea salt
1   cup strawberries, hulled and thinly sliced

Pulse dates, nuts, oats, and sea salt in a food processor just until combined. Press mixture into the bottom of a 9-by-5-inch loaf pan.

Mash half the strawberries with a fork or potato masher, and spread on top of date mixture. Top with remaining strawberries. Slice into rectangles to serve. *Makes 6*

VEGAN DAIRY-FREE

PER SERVING (1 BAR) 176 CALORIES, 4 G FAT (1 G SATURATED FAT), 0 MG CHOLESTEROL, 36 G CARBOHYDRATES, 2 G PROTEIN, 4 G FIBER

roasted plums with yogurt and granola

¼   cup honey
⅓   cup fresh orange juice
4   large purple or red plums (about 1½ pounds), halved and pitted
     Plain yogurt, for serving
     Granola, preferably homemade (see recipe, page 101), for serving

Preheat oven to 400°F. Stir to combine honey and orange juice in an 8-inch square baking dish. Arrange plums, cut side down, in dish. Roast until tender and juicy, 25 to 30 minutes, turning plums over during final 10 minutes of baking and spooning juices over fruit. (If liquid evaporates completely during baking, add 1 to 2 tablespoons water.)

Serve plums warm or at room temperature, drizzled with pan juices and topped with yogurt and granola. *Serves 4*

PER SERVING 199 CALORIES, 3 G FAT (1 G SATURATED FAT), 1 MG CHOLESTEROL, 44 G CARBOHYDRATES, 3 G PROTEIN, 3 G FIBER

chocolate Everyone knows by now that dark chocolate (with at least 70 percent cacao) is filled with antioxidants. What follows are a few of our favorite ways to get our chocolate fix—besides simply unwrapping a bar.

coconut-chocolate macaroons

dark chocolate bark with hazelnuts

dark chocolate
truffles

dark
chocolate
"pudding"

dark chocolate bark with hazelnuts

Canola oil, for baking pan

8   ounces dark chocolate (at least 70 percent cacao), melted

¼   cup hazelnuts, blanched and toasted (see page 314), chopped

¼   teaspoon flaky sea salt, such as Maldon

Lightly brush an 8-inch square baking pan with oil. Line with parchment, leaving overhang. Pour in chocolate, and smooth into an even layer with an offset spatula.

Sprinkle evenly with hazelnuts and sea salt. Refrigerate until completely set, about 30 minutes. To serve, peel off parchment, and break into pieces. *Serves 6 to 8*

Note: Try different combinations of toppings: nuts, dried fruit, unsweetened coconut, grated orange zest, or candied ginger.

VEGAN DAIRY-FREE GLUTEN-FREE

PER SERVING 188 CALORIES, 16 G FAT (7 G SATURATED FAT), 0 MG CHOLESTEROL, 17 G CARBOHYDRATES, 3 G PROTEIN, 3 G FIBER

coconut-chocolate macaroons

1   large egg white

2   tablespoons honey

¼   teaspoon pure vanilla extract
    Grated zest of 1 lemon

⅛   teaspoon coarse salt

1½ cups finely shredded unsweetened coconut

2   ounces dark chocolate (at least 70 percent cacao), melted

Preheat oven to 375°F. In a bowl, whisk together egg white, honey, vanilla, lemon zest, and salt. Stir in coconut until completely coated with egg mixture. With a 1½-inch ice-cream scoop, make 15 balls, transferring each one to a parchment-lined baking sheet, spacing about 2 inches apart.

Bake, rotating halfway through, until coconut starts to turn golden brown on edges, about 12 minutes. Transfer sheet to a wire rack, and let cool completely. (Cookies can be stored in an airtight container up to 3 days.) Before serving, drizzle with melted chocolate, or dip one side in melted chocolate. Refrigerate 15 minutes to set. *Makes 15*

DAIRY-FREE NUT-FREE GLUTEN-FREE

PER SERVING (1 COOKIE) 97 CALORIES, 8 G FAT (6 G SATURATED FAT), 14 MG CHOLESTEROL, 6 G CARBOHYDRATES, 1 G PROTEIN, 1 G FIBER

dark chocolate "pudding"

3   avocados, halved, pitted, and peeled

¼   cup plus 2 tablespoons unsweetened cocoa powder

¼   cup honey

1   teaspoon pure vanilla extract

Flaky sea salt, such as Maldon, for serving

Puree avocados, cocoa, honey, and vanilla in a food processor or blender until smooth. Sprinkle with sea salt before serving. *Serves 4*

DAIRY-FREE **NUT-FREE GLUTEN-FREE**

<u>PER SERVING</u> 326 CALORIES, 23 G FAT (4 G SATURATED FAT), 0 MG CHOLESTEROL, 35 G CARBOHYDRATES, 5 G PROTEIN, 13 G FIBER

dark chocolate truffles

8   ounces dark chocolate (at least 70 percent cacao), chopped

¼   cup coconut oil

3   tablespoons water

1   teaspoon pure vanilla extract

Pinch of sea salt

¼   cup unsweetened cocoa powder, for rolling

Assorted toppings: cocoa powder, finely chopped nuts (pistachios, almonds, hazelnuts), and toasted unsweetened shredded coconut (see page 314)

Melt chocolate with oil and the water. Stir in vanilla and sea salt. Transfer to an 8-inch square baking dish, and refrigerate until mixture is set but still pliable, about 2 hours.

With a 1-inch ice-cream scoop, make 28 balls, transferring each one to a parchment-lined baking sheet. Coat hands in cocoa, and roll balls to make smooth. Refrigerate on sheet 10 minutes. (Truffles can be refrigerated in an airtight container up to 2 weeks; let stand at room temperature 30 minutes before coating.) To serve, roll in cocoa or pat with nuts or coconut. *Makes 28*

VEGAN DAIRY-FREE **NUT-FREE GLUTEN-FREE**

<u>PER SERVING</u> (3 TRUFFLES) 188 CALORIES, 15 G FAT (10 G SATURATED FAT), 0 MG CHOLESTEROL, 17 G CARBOHYDRATES, 1 G PROTEIN, 2 G FIBER

frozen Chill out! A frozen treat doesn't have to mean lots of refined sugar and heavy cream. These four easy recipes deliver all kinds of indulgence—and fresh fruit flavor, too.

watermelon-lime granita

frozen bananas with **cocoa**

coconut-water
ice pops

mixed berry
"sorbet"

frozen bananas with cocoa

1 ripe banana, peeled
3 tablespoons unsweetened cocoa powder
   Pinch of ground cinnamon

Cut banana on the bias into 4 pieces. Freeze on a plate, about 2 hours. Combine cocoa and cinnamon in a shallow dish; dip 1 side of each banana piece in mixture just before serving.
Serves 1

watermelon-lime granita

7 cups chopped seedless watermelon (from about one-third whole melon)
¼ cup honey
2 tablespoons fresh lime juice

Pulse watermelon, honey, and lime juice in a food processor until smooth. Pour into an 8-inch square glass baking dish, cover tightly, and freeze until set, about 6 hours or overnight. To serve, scrape with a fork into bowls.
Serves 8

VEGAN DAIRY-FREE
NUT-FREE GLUTEN-FREE

PER SERVING 142 CALORIES, 3 G FAT (1 G SATURATED FAT), 0 MG CHOLESTEROL, 36 G CARBOHYDRATES, 4 G PROTEIN, 9 G FIBER

DAIRY-FREE NUT-FREE GLUTEN-FREE

PER SERVING 65 CALORIES, 0 G FAT (0 G SATURATED FAT), 0 MG CHOLESTEROL, 17 G CARBOHYDRATES, 1 G PROTEIN, 1 G FIBER

mixed berry "sorbet"

3 ripe bananas, peeled and chopped
1 cup mixed berries, frozen

Freeze bananas on a plate, about 2 hours. Puree with berries in a food processor until smooth. Serve immediately. *Serves 2*

coconut-water ice pops

1 cup chopped fresh peeled mango, papaya, pineapple, or kiwi
¾ cup unsweetened coconut water
2 tablespoons honey

Puree fruit, coconut water, and honey in a blender until smooth. Transfer to frozen-pop molds, dividing evenly. Freeze until firm, 1 to 2 hours or up to 2 weeks. *Makes 5*

VEGAN DAIRY-FREE
NUT-FREE GLUTEN-FREE

PER SERVING 188 CALORIES, 1 G FAT (0 G SATURATED FAT), 0 MG CHOLESTEROL, 49 G CARBOHYDRATES, 2 G PROTEIN, 7 G FIBER

DAIRY-FREE NUT-FREE GLUTEN-FREE

PER SERVING (1 POP) 130 CALORIES, 9 G FAT (8 G SATURATED FAT), 0 MG CHOLESTEROL, 15 G CARBOHYDRATES, 1 G PROTEIN, 1 G FIBER

baked Take your pick of textures—crisp and crunchy, soft and chewy, or chunky and nutty. You'll find them here, along with wholesome ingredients that make these treats all the sweeter.

fig and **walnut**
biscotti

berry-almond
crisp

chocolate-
walnut brownies

oatmeal-raisin
cookies

fig and walnut biscotti

1¾ cups whole-wheat flour

¾ cup packed dark-brown sugar

2 teaspoons baking powder

¾ teaspoon coarse salt

¾ teaspoon anise seeds, chopped

3 large eggs

1 tablespoon finely grated orange zest

1 cup coarsely chopped dried figs (6 ounces)

1 cup walnuts, toasted (page 314) and chopped

Preheat oven to 325°F. Whisk together flour, brown sugar, baking powder, salt, and anise. With an electric mixer, whisk eggs until thick enough to hold a ribbon for 1 second when whisk is lifted, about 5 minutes. Whisk in zest. Fold egg mixture into flour mixture; fold in figs and walnuts. Divide dough in half; form each piece into a 2½-inch-wide log on a parchment-lined baking sheet, 3 inches apart.

Bake until almost firm, about 25 minutes. Let cool on sheet 10 minutes. Reduce oven heat to 300°F. Slice logs on the diagonal ½ inch thick; arrange slices on sheet. Bake until golden, about 14 minutes, flipping halfway through. Let cool on a wire rack. *Makes 30*

DAIRY-FREE

PER SERVING (2 COOKIES) 184 CALORIES, 6 G FAT (1 G SATURATED FAT), 42 MG CHOLESTEROL, 30 G CARBOHYDRATES, 5 G PROTEIN, 3 G FIBER

berry-almond crisp

For Topping

½ cup old-fashioned rolled oats

¼ cup spelt flour

¼ cup maple sugar or light-brown sugar

½ teaspoon ground cinnamon

3 tablespoons coconut oil, melted

2 teaspoons pure maple syrup

1½ teaspoons pure vanilla extract

½ cup almonds, toasted (page 314) and chopped

For Filling

6 cups mixed berries (1 pound 14 ounces)

½ teaspoon ground cinnamon

1 tablespoon arrowroot or cornstarch

2 tablespoons pure maple syrup

1 teaspoon finely grated orange zest

1 teaspoon pure vanilla extract

Plain Greek yogurt, for serving (optional)

Preheat oven to 350°F. Combine topping and filling ingredients in separate bowls. Pour filling into a 9-inch pie plate; sprinkle with topping. Bake on a parchment-lined rimmed baking sheet until topping is golden, about 50 minutes. Serve warm with yogurt, if desired. *Serves 6*

VEGAN DAIRY-FREE

PER SERVING 324 CALORIES, 14 G FAT (6 G SATURATED FAT), 0 MG CHOLESTEROL, 48 G CARBOHYDRATES, 5 G PROTEIN, 6 G FIBER

chocolate-walnut brownies

⅓ cup extra-virgin olive oil, plus more for brushing

8 ounces dark chocolate (at least 70 percent cacao), chopped

⅓ cup light-brown sugar

⅓ cup pure maple syrup

2 large eggs

2 tablespoons unsweetened cocoa powder

½ teaspoon baking soda

¼ teaspoon coarse salt

⅔ cup almond flour

½ cup coarsely chopped walnuts

Preheat oven to 350°F. Brush an 8-inch square baking pan with oil. Line with parchment, leaving overhang. Brush parchment with oil.

Melt half of chocolate in a heatproof bowl; whisk in oil, sugar, and syrup. Remove from heat. Whisk in eggs, one at a time, then cocoa, baking soda, and salt. Fold in flour and remaining chocolate. Pour batter into prepared pan; sprinkle with walnuts. Bake until a toothpick comes out clean, about 30 minutes. Let cool completely on a wire rack. To serve, cut into 2-inch squares. *Makes 16*

DAIRY-FREE GLUTEN-FREE

PER SERVING (1 BROWNIE) 206 CALORIES, 16 G FAT (4 G SATURATED FAT), 26 MG CHOLESTEROL, 17 G CARBOHYDRATES, 3 G PROTEIN, 2 G FIBER

oatmeal-raisin cookies

1 cup whole-wheat flour

½ cup toasted wheat germ

1 teaspoon baking soda

1 teaspoon ground cinnamon

½ teaspoon coarse salt

⅔ cup safflower or canola oil

¾ cup packed dark-brown sugar

2 large eggs

1 teaspoon pure vanilla extract

2½ cups old-fashioned rolled oats

1 cup raisins

Preheat oven to 325°F. Whisk flour, wheat germ, baking soda, cinnamon, and salt. In another bowl, whisk oil, brown sugar, eggs, and vanilla. Stir flour mixture into egg mixture; mix in oats and raisins. Roll 2 tablespoons of dough into a ball; repeat. Place on parchment-lined baking sheets, 2 inches apart. Bake until golden brown, 10 to 13 minutes. Let cool on sheets 5 minutes; let cool completely on a wire rack. *Makes 2 dozen*

DAIRY-FREE NUT-FREE

PER SERVING (1 COOKIE) 174 CALORIES, 6 G FAT (0 G SATURATED FAT), 18 MG CHOLESTEROL, 28 G CARBOHYDRATES, 4 G PROTEIN, 2 G FIBER

drinks Rethink what it means to end a meal on a sweet note. A sip of something rich, soothing, and soul-satisfying can leave you feeling very relaxed, indeed.

almond-cinnamon frappé

spiced **hot**
dark chocolate

spiced **apple cider**

chai tea latte

spiced
hot dark chocolate

1 quart almond milk, preferably homemade (see recipe, page 315)

6 ounces dark chocolate (at least 70 percent cacao), chopped

½ teaspoon ground cinnamon

⅛ to ¼ teaspoon ground cardamom, to taste

⅛ teaspoon cayenne pepper

⅛ teaspoon coarse salt

Heat all ingredients in a small saucepan over medium-low, whisking constantly, until chocolate has melted and mixture is steaming, about 5 minutes. Serve immediately. *Serves 4*

almond-cinnamon frappé

2 tablespoons almond butter (see recipe, page 315)

1 cup almond milk, preferably homemade (see recipe, page 315)

1 tablespoon honey

¼ teaspoon ground cinnamon, plus more for sprinkling

Blend all ingredients in a blender until frothy. Serve over ice, sprinkled with cinnamon. *Serves 1*

VEGAN DAIRY-FREE
NUT-FREE GLUTEN-FREE

PER SERVING 277 CALORIES, 21 G FAT (9 G SATURATED FAT), 0 MG CHOLESTEROL, 30 G CARBOHYDRATES, 4 G PROTEIN, 4 G FIBER

DAIRY-FREE GLUTEN-FREE

PER SERVING 327 CALORIES, 21 G FAT (2 G SATURATED FAT), 0 MG CHOLESTEROL, 33 G CARBOHYDRATES, 6 G PROTEIN, 3 G FIBER

chai tea latte

2   whole cardamom pods, lightly crushed
⅛   teaspoon whole black peppercorns
2   whole cloves
1   cinnamon stick
1   piece (1½ inches) fresh ginger, peeled and thinly sliced
2   cups water
2   tablespoons packed light-brown sugar
2   bags black tea, such as Assam or Darjeeling
¾   cup milk (dairy, almond, or coconut)

Bring spices, ginger, and the water to a boil in a small saucepan. Reduce heat and simmer until fragrant, about 15 minutes. Whisk in brown sugar, then add tea bags; turn off heat, and let steep 3 minutes.

Strain tea mixture through a fine sieve into serving pot. Heat milk over medium until just simmering, then remove from heat and whisk until frothy. Pour into serving pot, stirring to combine. Serve immediately. *Serves 2*

GLUTEN-FREE

PER SERVING 91 CALORIES, 1 G FAT (0 G SATURATED FAT), 5 MG CHOLESTEROL, 18 G CARBOHYDRATES, 3 G PROTEIN, 0 G FIBER

spiced apple cider

1   quart unfiltered apple cider
8   allspice berries
4   whole cardamom pods
3   whole cloves
3   strips (about 2 inches wide) orange zest
2   cinnamon sticks, plus more for garnish (optional)

Heat all ingredients in a medium saucepan over medium; simmer until fragrant, about 5 minutes. Cider can be kept warm over very low heat. Strain before serving, and garnish with cinnamon sticks, if desired. *Serves 4*

VEGAN DAIRY-FREE
NUT-FREE GLUTEN-FREE

PER SERVING 121 CALORIES, 0 G FAT (0 G SATURATED FAT), 0 MG CHOLESTEROL, 30 G CARBOHYDRATES, 0 G PROTEIN, 0 G FIBER

basics

TOASTING NUTS, SEEDS, AND COCONUT

To toast nuts such as almonds, walnuts, or pecans: Spread them on a rimmed baking sheet and bake at 350°F until fragrant, tossing once or twice, about 10 minutes. (Start checking after 6 minutes if toasting sliced or chopped nuts.)

PINE NUTS AND SEEDS

Bake pine nuts at 350°F for 5 to 7 minutes, and pepitas (pumpkin seeds) or sunflower seeds at 300°F for about 12 minutes, or until lightly browned.

HAZELNUTS

Bake at 375°F until skins split, 10 to 12 minutes; when cool enough to handle, rub warm nuts in a clean kitchen towel to remove skins.

SESAME SEEDS

Toast in a skillet over medium heat, shaking the pan occasionally, until golden, 2 to 3 minutes (be careful not to let them burn).

COCONUT

Spread coconut in a single layer on a rimmed baking sheet, and bake at 350°F until starting to brown, tossing occasionally, 5 to 10 minutes.

ROASTING PEPPERS OR CHILES

Roast peppers or chiles (such as poblanos) over a gas flame, turning with tongs, until charred all over. Transfer to a bowl, cover with a large plate, and let stand until cool enough to handle. Scrape off skins with a paring knife. (Do not run roasted peppers under water.) Remove and discard stems, ribs, and seeds.

SEGMENTING CITRUS

Use a paring knife to cut peel and pith away from citrus, following curve of the fruit. Working over a bowl, cut between membranes, allowing segments to fall into bowl. Discard membranes.

PRESSING TOFU

Arrange tofu on a baking sheet lined with a double layer of paper towels, then top with another double layer of paper towels and another baking sheet. Weight with a heavy skillet or canned goods to press out excess liquid, about 20 minutes.

CLEANSING BROTH

Makes 8 cups

- 1 large onion, chopped
- 6 carrots, peeled and chopped
- ¼ head celery, chopped
- 1 head garlic, halved
- 2 large sweet potatoes, chopped
- 12 cups water
- 4 cups spinach
- 1 bunch fresh flat-leaf parsley
   Coarse salt and freshly ground pepper

In a stockpot, bring onion, carrots, celery, garlic, sweet potatoes, and the water to a boil. Reduce heat; simmer 20 minutes. Add spinach and parsley; simmer 5 minutes. Season with salt and pepper. Pour through a fine sieve; discard solids. The stock can be refrigerated up to 5 days or frozen for up to 3 months; thaw in the refrigerator before using.

CHICKEN STOCK

Makes about 2½ quarts

- 5 pounds chicken parts (backs, necks, and wings)
- 2 medium carrots, peeled and chopped
- 2 celery stalks, chopped
- 2 medium onions, peeled and cut into eighths
- 1 dried bay leaf
- 1 teaspoon whole black peppercorns

Place chicken parts in a stockpot, and add enough water to cover by 1 inch (about 3 quarts). Bring to a boil, skimming foam with a ladle as it rises to the surface.

Add vegetables, bay leaf, and peppercorns and reduce heat to a bare simmer. Cook, skimming frequently, 1½ to 2½ hours (depending on taste preference).

Pass through a fine sieve; discard solids. Skim off fat if using immediately, or let cool completely before transferring to airtight containers. Refrigerate at least 8 hours to allow the fat to accumulate at the top; lift off and discard fat. The stock can be refrigerated up to 3 days or frozen up to 3 months; thaw in the refrigerator before using.

VEGETABLE STOCK

Makes 6 cups

This stock freezes well, so you may want to make a couple of batches (just double the recipe) to use in all your vegetarian cooking. To crush peppercorns, press with the bottom of a small skillet; or crush with the side of a large knife on a cutting board.

2 leeks, white and light-green parts only, cut into 1-inch rounds and rinsed well

2 carrots, peeled and chopped

1 small onion, chopped

3 garlic cloves

8 cups water

5 sprigs flat-leaf parsley

2 sprigs thyme

1 dried bay leaf

2 teaspoons whole black peppercorns, crushed

Combine leeks, carrots, onion, and garlic in a stockpot. Cover; cook over medium heat, stirring occasionally, for 10 minutes.

Add the water, herbs, and peppercorns. Bring to a boil. Reduce heat, and simmer 30 minutes. Pour through a fine sieve; discard solids. The stock can be refrigerated up to 2 days or frozen for up to 3 months; thaw in the refrigerator before using.

FISH STOCK
Makes about 2 quarts

2 tablespoons sunflower or safflower oil

2 pounds fish bones and heads

1 celery stalk, chopped

1 leek, white and light-green parts only, cut into 1-inch rounds and rinsed well

1 cup dry white wine

1 dried bay leaf

5 whole black peppercorns

Heat oil in a stockpot over medium until hot but not smoking. Add fish parts, celery, and leek. Cover and cook, stirring occasionally, until vegetables are soft and fish has turned opaque, about 3 minutes.

Add wine and reduce by half, 3 to 5 minutes. Add enough water to cover by ½ inch (about 2 quarts), along with the bay leaf and peppercorns. Bring to just under a boil, skimming foam with a ladle as it rises to the surface. Reduce heat and gently simmer for 35 minutes, skimming frequently.

Pass mixture through a fine sieve; discard solids. Skim off fat. If not using immediately, let cool completely before transferring to airtight containers. The stock can be refrigerated up to 2 days or frozen for up to 3 months; thaw in the refrigerator before using.

HARISSA
Makes ⅓ cup

1 tablespoon whole cumin seeds

1 tablespoon whole coriander seeds

1 tablespoon whole caraway seeds

1 teaspoon cayenne pepper

1 garlic clove, crushed

2 tablespoons fresh lemon juice

Large pinch of sea salt

¼ cup extra-virgin olive oil

Warm a skillet over medium heat. Add cumin, coriander, and caraway seeds. Toast, shaking pan, until seeds are fragrant, about 3 minutes. Grind in a spice grinder until fine.

Place ground spices in a bowl and add cayenne, garlic, lemon juice, and salt. Stir in olive oil until smooth. Refrigerate in a glass jar up to 1 month.

ALMOND MILK
Makes 3½ cups

1 cup whole raw almonds

4 cups water

½ teaspoon pure vanilla extract

Place almonds in a blender. Bring 1 cup water to a boil; pour over almonds. Let stand 30 minutes. Add remaining 3 cups water and vanilla; blend until frothy. Pour through a fine sieve into a bowl and discard solids. Almond milk can be stored in an airtight container in the refrigerator up to 5 days. Shake before serving.

ALMOND BUTTER
Makes 1 cup

2 cups whole raw almonds, toasted (see below)

1 teaspoon coarse salt

Process almonds in a food processor, scraping down sides, until smooth and creamy, 8 to 10 minutes. Season with salt. Almond butter can be stored in an airtight container in the refrigerator up to 5 days. Stir before serving.

sources

The following is a list of the trusted vendors, providers, and organizations our editors turn to most often for supplies, ingredients, and information.

TOOLS AND EQUIPMENT

Breville
866-273-8455
www.brevilleusa.com

Juicers and blenders

Macy's
800-289-6229
macys.com

Juicers, blenders, food processors, salad spinners, steamers, and general cooking equipment

Sur La Table
800-243-0852
www.surlatable.com

Juicers, blenders, food processors, salad spinners, steamers, and general cooking equipment

Williams-Sonoma
800-840-2591
www.williams-sonoma.com

Juicers, blenders, food processors, salad spinners, steamers, and general cooking equipment

The Wok Shop
888-780-7171
www.wokshop.com

Steamers and woks

INGREDIENTS

Anson Mills
803-467-4122
www.ansonmills.com

Organic whole grains, whole-grain and gluten-free flours (rice and buckwheat)

Arrowhead Mills
800-434-4246
www.arrowheadmills.com

Whole grains, dried legumes, flaxseeds, organic whole-grain and gluten-free flours, and tahini

Bob's Red Mill
800-349-2173
www.bobsredmill.com

Whole grains (including barley and spelt flakes), whole-grain and gluten-free flours, dried beans and legumes, and seeds (including flaxseeds and chia seeds), plus unsweetened coconut flakes

Copper River Seafoods
907-522-7806
www.copperriverseafoods.com

Wild Alaskan salmon, shrimp, halibut, black cod, and Pacific cod

ImportFood.com
888-618-8424
www.importfood.com

Asian produce (including fresh lemongrass), spices, and fish sauce

Kalustyan's
212-685-3451
www.kalustyans.com

Dried beans and legumes, whole grains, whole-wheat and gluten-free flours, Asian noodles, spices, seasonings (including harissa and sambal oelek), and sea salts

Nuts.com
800-558-6887
www.nuts.com

Raw nuts, seeds (including chia seeds and flaxseeds), nut and seed butters (including sunflower-seed butter and tahini), unsweetened dried fruits, whole grains, and gluten-free flours

Penzeys
800-741-7787
www.penzeys.com

Spices, herbs, seasonings, and sea salts

Rancho Gordo
707-259-1935
www.ranchogordo.com

Heirloom dried beans and legumes, whole grains, chiles and chile powders, and spices

Spectrum Organics
800-434-4246
www.spectrumorganics.com

Organic cooking oils (including avocado, coconut, grapeseed, walnut, and toasted sesame oils) and vinegars

Wild Planet
800-301-3270
www.wildplanetfoods.com

Sustainably canned seafood, including anchovies, salmon, sardines, and tuna

RESOURCES

Animal Welfare Approved
www.animalwelfareapproved.org

Information and guidelines on food labeling; listing of AWA farmers, co-ops, and other food purveyors

Center for Food Safety
www.centerforfoodsafety.org

Information on organic and sustainable food and products

The Center for Mindful Eating
www.tcme.org

Principles of mindful eating

Center for Science in the Public Interest
http://cspinet.org/index.html

Research and information on health and nutrition

The Cornucopia Institute
www.cornucopia.org

Research and information on organic foods and products

Eat Wild
www.eatwild.com

Information about pasture-based farming and a state-by-state directory of farmers who sell directly to consumers

Environmental Working Group
www.ewg.org

News and information on food and food policy

Harvard School of Public Health's Healthy Eating Plate
www.hsph.harvard.edu/
nutritionsource/healthy-eating-plate

Guidance on healthy eating choices

Humane Farm Animal Care
www.certifiedhumane.org

Searchable database of certified humane products (eggs, dairy, and meat) and food service distributors

Institute of Medicine of the National Academies (IOM)
www.iom.edu

Information and advice concerning health policy

LocalHarvest
www.localharvest.org

Database of farmer's markets, greenmarkets, and Community Supported Agriculture (CSA), searchable by location

Monterey Bay Aquarium
www.seafoodwatch.org

Information and recommendations for buying seafood

National Oceanic and Atmospheric Administration (NOAA)
www.fishwatch.gov

News and science relating to sustainable seafood, with profiles for each variety harvested in the United States

Natural Resources Defense Council
www.nrdc.org

Guidelines for making healthy food choices

Nutrition Data
http://nutritiondata.self.com

Information and advice on healthy eating, plus interactive tools for determining the nutritional content of foods

Oldways—the Food Issues Think Tank
www.oldwaysspt.org

Guidance on mindful eating, stocking your kitchen, reading food labels, and cooking healthful meals

SlowFoodUSA
www.slowfoodusa.org

Advocacy and advice on preparing fresh, wholesome, clean food

United States Department of Agriculture (USDA)
www.usda.gov

Nutritional guidelines and information and a searchable database of Community Supported Agriculture (CSA) by location

U.S. Food and Drug Administration (FDA)
www.fda.gov

Information and guidance on food labeling and nutrition

Whole Grains Council
www.wholegrainscouncil.org

Guidance on health benefits of whole grains

acknowledgments

For this, our eighty-third book, we are grateful for the contributions of so many talented colleagues. A big thank you to food editor Shira Bocar, who developed foolproof recipes as well as offered helpful insight and superb food styling, and to the other MSLO food editors, past and present, who provided recipes and ideas to the book.

Special thanks to executive editor Evelyn Battaglia and editorial director Ellen Morrissey for their expertise in shaping the content into a meaningful, unified whole, and managing editor Susanne Ruppert for keeping everything in great shape and on schedule. Design director Jennifer Wagner created the clean, elegant, modern design that presents the text, recipes, and photographs in a clear, easy-to-follow format. John Myers compiled the voluminous photographs and provided invaluable production assistance along with Denise Clappi, Kiyomi Marsh, and Alison Vanek Devine.

As always, thank you to MSLO chief content director Eric A. Pike for his priceless input, and executive editorial director of food Lucinda Scala Quinn and editorial director Jennifer Aaronson for continuing to lead the MSLO food team in producing a wealth of recipes to work with. Others who contributed to the book include Claudine Eriksson, Laura Loesch-Quintin, Nicole Coppola, Pam Morris, and Felicia Sanabria.

An authoritative guide like this requires careful oversight, and Kathie Madonna Swift, M.S., R.D., L.D.N., lent her extensive expertise in vetting all the information contained herein and being an essential source of guidance along the way. Christine Cyr Clisset also conducted much of the research.

Thanks to photographer Johnny Miller, who provided the bulk of the beautiful images in this book, and to the other talented photographers whose work appear on these pages (see the complete list, opposite).

We are ever grateful to our longtime partners at Clarkson Potter, especially publisher Pam Krauss, associate publisher Doris Cooper, creative director Marysarah Quinn, art director Jane Treuhaft, production director Linnea Knollmueller, managing editor Sally Franklin, senior production editor Patricia Shaw, associate editor Jessica Freeman-Slade, and editors Emily Takoudes, Ashley Phillips, and Angelin Borsics. Thanks as well to Carly Gorga, Maha Kahlil, Maya Mavjee, Donna Passannante, and Kate Tyler.

photo credits

Sang An page 259

Christopher Baker pages 149, 156

Jennifer Causey pages 77, 275

Bryan Gardner pages 63, 91, 103, 133, 158, 162, 195 (left), 199 (right), 203 (left), 205 (left), 207 (left), 209 (left), 211, 231, 236, 248, 277, 281

William Hereford page 177

Raymond Hom pages 85, 126, 142, 155, 197 (right), 221, 228, 251, 261, 272, 289

Ditte Isager page 199 (left)

John Kernick pages 146, 161, 247

Yunhee Kim page 139

Ryan Liebe pages 135, 175, 263

Andrew McCaul pages 88, 222

Kate Mathis page 195 (right)

Johnny Miller pages 1–5, 9, 10–11, 38, 40, 42, 44, 70–73, 74, 78, 81, 82, 99, 100, 105, 107, 108–119, 121, 123, 125, 129, 130, 151, 153, 165, 167, 168, 171, 172, 181, 182, 184–187, 191, 193, 197 (left), 201, 203 (right), 207 (right), 209 (right), 212–213, 215, 219, 225, 227, 233, 240, 244, 253, 256, 267, 268, 271, 279, 285, 287, 291–295, 298–299, 302–303, 306–307, 310–311, 336

Marcus Nilsson pages 145, 216, 235

Con Poulos page 178

Maria Robledo page 87

Emily Kate Roemer pages 93, 205 (right)

Anson Smart page 94

Christopher Testani page 239

Romulo Yanes pages 136, 141, 242, 254, 264, 282

recipe index

BREAKFAST

RECIPES	V	DF	NF	GF
Banana-Apple Buckwheat Muffins, *p. 90*		●		●
Barley with Apricots, Hazelnuts, Chocolate, and Honey, *p. 97*				
Black Quinoa with Avocado, Almonds, and Honey, *p. 96*		●		●
Breakfast Vegetable-Miso Soup with Chickpeas, *p. 102*	●	●	●	●
Cardamom Quinoa Porridge with Pear, *p. 104*	●	●		●
Coconut Breakfast Pudding with Sautéed Nectarines, *p. 76*	●	●		
Crostini with Fresh Ricotta, Cherries, and Lemon Zest, *p. 84*			●	
Frittata with Spring Vegetables, *p. 79*		●	●	●
Fruit and Almond Alpine Muesli, *p. 89*				
Honey-Caramelized Figs with Yogurt, *p. 83*				●
Millet with Pineapple, Coconut, and Flaxseed, *p. 95*	●	●		●
Mixed-Grain and Almond Granola, *p.101*				
Mushroom and Microgreen Omelet, *p. 106*		●	●	●
Poached Eggs with Roasted Tomatoes, *p. 98*		●	●	
Sardines and Cream Cheese on Rye, *p. 92*			●	
Steamed Salmon with Avocado, *p. 80*		●	●	
Tofu Scramble with Cotija Cheese and Tortillas, *p. 86*			●	●
Whole-Wheat Waffles with Sliced Strawberries and Yogurt, *p. 75*			●	

DRINKS

RECIPES	V	DF	NF	GF
Almond Cinnamon Frappé, *p. 312*		●		●
Almond-Date Smoothie, *p. 114*				●
Aloe-Vera, Ginger, and Orange Smoothie, *p. 117*		●	●	●
Apple, Cucumber, and Lemon Juice, *p. 110*	●	●	●	●
Avocado-Yogurt Smoothie, *p. 114*			●	●
Beet, Apple, and Mint Juice, *p. 111*	●	●	●	●
Blackberry-Plum Smoothie, *p. 113*	●	●	●	●
Blueberry–Green Tea Smoothie, *p. 113*		●	●	●
Blueberry-Yogurt Smoothie, *p. 114*				●

Recipe	V	DF	NF	GF
Chai Tea Latte, *p. 313*				●
Coconut-Cherry Smoothie, *p. 112*	●	●	●	●
Cucumber-Pear Juice, *p. 116*	●	●	●	●
Grapefruit, Carrot, and Ginger Juice, *p. 111*	●	●	●	●
Green Goodness Juice, *p. 112*	●	●	●	●
Green Machine Smoothie, *p. 111*	●	●	●	●
Mango–Coconut Water Smoothie, *p. 116*	●	●	●	●
Melon-Mint Smoothie, *p. 116*		●	●	●
Mixed Berry–Tofu Smoothie, *p. 115*	●	●	●	●
Pear, Oat, and Ginger Smoothie, *p. 115*				●
Pineapple-Spinach Juice, *p. 117*	●	●	●	●
Spiced Apple Cider, *p. 313*	●	●	●	●
Spiced Hot Dark Chocolate, *p. 312*	●	●	●	●
Spiced Papaya Smoothie, *p. 112*		●	●	●
Spinach-Apple Juice, *p. 113*	●	●	●	●
Strawberry, Grapefruit, and Ginger Smoothie, *p. 110*	●	●	●	●
Sweet Kale-Sunflower Smoothie, *p. 115*		●	●	●
Ultra-Green Juice, *p. 110*	●	●	●	●
Watermelon-Ginger Juice, *p. 117*	●	●	●	●

SOUPS AND STEWS

RECIPES	V	DF	NF	GF
Almond Chicken Soup with Sweet Potato, Collards, and Ginger, *p. 288*		●		●
Avocado, Radish, and Basil Soup, *p. 164*	●	●	●	●
Beet and Buttermilk Soup, *p. 128*			●	●
Bell Pepper, Yogurt, and Harissa Soup, *p. 164*			●	●
Breakfast Vegetable-Miso Soup with Chickpeas, *p. 102*	●	●	●	●
Broccoli-Spinach Soup with Avocado Toasts, *p. 157*			●	
Buckwheat Noodles, Bok Choy, and Sweet Potatoes in Miso-Lime Broth, *p. 144*	●	●	●	
Carrot, Spinach, and Green Bean Soup with Dill, *p. 183*	●	●	●	●
Creamy Summer Squash Soup with Cilantro, *p. 173*	●	●	●	●
Cucumber and Yogurt Soup, *p. 128*			●	●
Dashi-Poached Sweet Potatoes and Greens, *p. 137*		●	●	●
Mediterranean Chicken Stew with Couscous, *p. 252*		●	●	
Poached Chicken with Bok Choy in Ginger Broth, *p. 232*		●	●	●

	V	DF	NF	GF
Pureed Cauliflower Soup, *p. 152*		●	●	●
Red Lentil Soup with Turnip and Parsley, *p. 266*	●	●	●	●
Shrimp, Cod, and Fennel Soup with Tomatoes, *p. 274*		●	●	●
Spicy Indian Chicken and Tomato Soup, *p. 224*		●	●	●
Spicy North African Chicken-Chickpea Stew, *p. 273*		●	●	●
Watercress and Potato Soup, *p. 124*		●	●	●
White Bean, Potato, and Kale Stew, *p. 176*			●	●

SALADS

RECIPES	V	DF	NF	GF
Beet, Avocado, and Arugula Salad with Sunflower Seeds, *p. 150*	●	●	●	●
Black Sea Bass with Barley, Shiitake, and Edamame Salad, *p. 241*		●	●	
Broccoli and Brown Rice Salad with Pumpkin Seeds, *p. 140*			●	●
Brussels Sprout Salad with Avocado and Pumpkin Seeds, *p. 154*	●	●	●	●
Bulgur Salad with Pomegranate Seeds, *p. 166*	●	●	●	
Citrus Salad with Pomegranate, *p. 296*	●	●	●	●
Farro, Pea Shoot, and Goat Cheese Salad, *p. 127*				
Farro and Roasted Sweet Potato Salad, *p. 174*	●	●	●	
Fennel, Sunchoke, and Green Apple Salad, *p. 122*		●		●
Grapefruit, Salmon, and Avocado Salad, *p. 265*		●	●	●
Grilled Chicken with Cherry and Arugula Salad, *p. 229*		●	●	●
Quinoa Salad with Zucchini, Mint, and Pistachios, *p. 134*	●	●		●
Roasted Golden-Beet, Avocado, and Watercress Salad, *p. 170*			●	●
Roasted Red-Pepper Salad with Anchovy White Beans, *p. 180*			●	●
Roasted Sweet Peppers and Carrots with Orange and Hazelnuts, *p. 148*				●
Sardine Salad with Lemon and Herbs, *p. 190*	●	●	●	●
Squash Salad with Tomatoes, Zucchini Blossoms, and Ricotta, *p. 138*			●	●
Steamed Vegetable Salad with Macadamia Dressing, *p. 179*		●		●
Swiss Chard Salad with Poached Egg, *p. 131*			●	●
Watercress, Sardine, and Orange Salad, *p. 280*		●	●	●
White Peach and Heirloom Tomato Salad, *p. 160*			●	●

MAIN DISHES

RECIPES	V	DF	NF	GF
Almond Chicken Soup with Sweet Potato, Collards, and Ginger, *p. 288*		●		●
Almond-Crusted Chicken Breast with Spinach, *p. 258*		●		●

Recipe	1	2	3	4
Baked Sweet Potato with Greens, *p. 132*	●	●	●	●
Barley with Brussels Sprouts, Spinach, and Edamame, *p. 143*	●	●		
Black Cod with Herbs, Zucchini, and Whole-Wheat Couscous, *p. 260*		●	●	
Black Sea Bass with Barley, Shiitake, and Edamame Salad, *p. 241*		●	●	
Brown Rice Cakes with Sautéed Fennel, Broccoli Rabe, and Ricotta, *p. 223*			●	●
Brown Rice with Salmon, Avocado, and Toasted Nori, *p. 286*		●	●	●
Buttermilk-Poached Chicken with Escarole and Radicchio, *p. 255*				●
Caramelized Fennel, Celery, and Sardine Pasta, *p. 246*		●	●	
Cauliflower "Rice" Stir-Fry with Pumpkin Seeds, *p. 163*	●	●	●	●
Chicken Paillards with Squash and Spinach, *p. 217*		●	●	●
Farro Spaghetti with Fresh Tomatoes and Marcona Almonds, *p. 257*	●	●		
Frittata with Spring Vegetables, *p. 79*		●	●	●
Ginger-Scallion Chicken Breasts in Parchment, *p. 284*		●	●	●
Grapefruit, Salmon, and Avocado Salad, *p. 265*		●	●	●
Grilled Chicken with Cherry and Arugula Salad, *p. 229*		●	●	●
Grilled Chicken with Cucumber, Radish, and Cherry Tomato Relish, *p. 245*		●	●	●
Grilled Salmon and Bok Choy with Orange-Avocado Salsa, *p. 276*		●	●	●
Grilled Tofu with Chimichurri on Toast, *p. 218*	●	●	●	
Lentil Burgers with Lettuce and Yogurt, *p. 243*			●	
Mediterranean Chicken Stew with Couscous, *p. 252*		●	●	
Moroccan-Steamed Salmon with Quinoa and Carrots, *p. 290*		●	●	●
Poached Chicken with Bok Choy in Ginger Broth, *p. 232*		●	●	●
Poached Egg with Rice and Edamame, *p. 230*		●	●	●
Poached Salmon with Fennel and Grapefruit, *p. 283*		●	●	●
Quesadillas with Collard Greens and White Beans, *p. 226*			●	
Red Lentil Soup with Turnip and Parsley, *p. 266*	●	●	●	●
Roasted Mushroom Tartines with Avocado, *p. 169*	●	●	●	
Roasted Portobellos with Kale and Red Onion, *p. 159*		●	●	●
Roasted Squash with Grains, Grapes, and Sage, *p. 147*	●	●	●	
Roasted Vegetables with Quinoa, *p. 120*	●	●	●	●
Sautéed Mushrooms with Toasted Flatbread and Baked Eggs, *p. 262*		●	●	
Seared Halibut Tacos with Grapefruit-Avocado Salsa, *p. 234*		●	●	●
Shiitake Mushrooms and Brown Rice in Parchment, *p. 249*	●	●	●	●
Shrimp, Cod, and Fennel Soup with Tomatoes, *p. 274*		●	●	●
Soba with Salmon and Watercress, *p. 214*			●	●

Recipes	V	DF	NF	GF
Spaghetti with Collard Greens and Lemon, *p. 269*				
Spicy Cauliflower, Bok Choy, and Shrimp Stir-Fry with Coconut, *p. 238*		●	●	●
Spicy Indian Chicken and Tomato Soup, *p. 224*		●	●	●
Spicy North African Chicken-Chickpea Stew, *p. 273*		●	●	●
Spinach, Tofu, and Brown Rice Bowl, *p. 237*	●	●	●	●
Spinach Tart with Olive-Oil Cracker Crust, *p. 278*			●	
Steamed Salmon with Avocado, *p. 80*		●	●	
Trout, Tomatoes, and Basil in Parchment, *p. 270*		●	●	●
Watercress, Sardine, and Orange Salad, *p. 280*		●	●	●
Wild Salmon, Asparagus, and Shiitakes in Parchment, *p. 220*		●	●	●
Wild Salmon with Lentils and Arugula, *p. 250*		●	●	●

SNACKS

Recipes	V	DF	NF	GF
Apple with Peanut Butter and Oats, *p. 206*	●	●		
Baked Apple Chips, *p. 196*	●	●	●	●
Dried Fruit and Nut Bites, *p. 210*	●	●		●
Frozen Grapes and Kiwi, *p. 202*	●	●	●	●
Garlic-Herb Yogurt Cheese, *p. 194*			●	●
Green Goddess Dip, *p. 200*			●	●
Hard-Cooked Eggs with Mustard, *p. 190*		●	●	●
Honey-Caramelized Figs with Yogurt, *p. 83*				●
Kale Chips with Sesame Seeds, *p. 194*	●	●	●	●
Melon with Feta and Black Pepper, *p. 208*			●	●
Mixed-Grain and Almond Granola, *p. 101*				
Pureed Pea Dip with Mint and Lemon, *p. 208*	●	●	●	●
Red Pepper and Walnut Dip with Pomegranate, *p. 189*	●	●		
Roasted Beet–White Bean Hummus, *p. 189*	●	●	●	●
Roasted Cauliflower Yogurt Dip, *p. 188*			●	●
Roasted Edamame with Cranberries, *p. 192*	●	●	●	●
Roasted Radishes and Greens, *p. 204*	●	●	●	●
Sardine Salad with Lemon and Herbs, *p. 190*	●	●	●	●
Simple Roasted Cauliflower, *p. 204*	●	●	●	●
Spiced Pumpkin Seeds, *p. 196*		●	●	●
Spicy Any-Bean Dip, *p. 188*	●	●	●	●

Recipe	V	DF	NF	GF
Spicy Yogurt and Cucumber Dip, *p. 200*			●	●
Steamed Green Beans with Lemon, *p. 198*	●	●	●	●
Sweet-Potato Chips, *p. 206*	●	●	●	●
Trail Mix with Toasted Coconut, *p. 210*	●	●		●
Tuna and White Beans, *p. 198*		●	●	●
Warm Spinach–White Bean Dip, *p. 192*			●	●
Watercress and Avocado Roll, *p. 202*	●	●	●	●

DESSERTS

RECIPES	V	DF	NF	GF
Almond-Cinnamon Frappé, *p. 312*		●		●
Berry-Almond Crisp, *p. 308*	●	●		
Chai Tea Latte, *p. 313*				●
Chocolate-Walnut Brownies, *p. 309*		●		●
Citrus Salad with Pomegranate, *p. 296*	●	●	●	●
Coconut-Chocolate Macaroons, *p. 300*		●	●	●
Coconut-Water Ice Pops, *p. 305*		●	●	●
Dark Chocolate Bark with Hazelnuts, *p. 300*	●	●		●
Dark Chocolate "Pudding," *p. 301*		●	●	●
Dark Chocolate Truffles, *p. 301*	●	●	●	●
Fig and Walnut Biscotti, *p. 308*		●		
Frozen Bananas with Cocoa, *p. 304*	●	●	●	●
Honey-Caramelized Figs with Yogurt, *p. 83*				●
Mixed Berry "Sorbet," *p. 305*	●	●	●	●
No-Bake Oat Bars with Strawberries, *p. 297*	●	●		
Oatmeal-Raisin Cookies, *p. 309*		●	●	
Pistachio-Stuffed Dates with Coconut, *p. 296*	●	●		●
Roasted Plums with Yogurt and Granola, *p. 297*				
Spiced Apple Cider, *p. 313*	●	●	●	●
Spiced Hot Dark Chocolate, *p. 312*	●	●	●	●
Watermelon-Lime Granita, *p. 304*		●	●	●

index

Note: Page references in *italics* indicate photographs.

A

Alcohol, 61
Allergies, 27, 37
Alliums, 39
Almond(s)
  Avocado, and Honey, Black Quinoa with, *94, 96*
  -Berry Crisp, *306,* 308
  Butter, 315
  Chicken Soup with Sweet Potato, Collards, and Ginger, 288, *289*
  -Cinnamon Frappé, *310, 312*
  -Crusted Chicken Breast with Spinach, 258, *259*
  -Date Smoothie, 114, *114*
  digestive benefits, 45
  and Fruit Alpine Muesli, 88, *89*
  healthy fats in, 58
  Marcona, and Fresh Tomatoes, Farro Spaghetti with, *256,* 257
  Milk, 315
  and Mixed-Grain Granola, *100,* 101
  Trail Mix with Toasted Coconut, 210, *211*
Aloe-Vera, Ginger, and Orange Smoothie, 117, *117*
Amaranth
  about, 50
  cooking methods, 51
Anchovy(ies)
  flavoring dishes with, 59
  Green Goddess Dip, 200, *201*
  Swiss Chard Salad with Poached Egg, *130,* 131
  White Beans, Roasted Red-Pepper Salad with, 180, *181*
Anti-inflammatory drinks, 112–13
Antioxidant foods, 41
Apple Cider, Spiced, *311,* 313

Apple(s)
  antioxidants in, 41
  -Banana Buckwheat Muffins, 90, *91*
  Beet, and Mint Juice, 111, *111*
  Chips, Baked, 196, *197*
  Cucumber, and Lemon Juice, 110, *110*
  Fruit and Almond Alpine Muesli, 88, 89
  Green, Sunchoke, and Fennel Salad, 122, *123*
  Green Goodness Juice, 112, *112*
  with Peanut Butter and Oats, 206, *207*
  -Spinach Juice, 113, *113*
  Sweet Kale-Sunflower Smoothie, 115, *115*
  Ultra-Green Juice, 110, *110*
Apricots
  Hazelnuts, Chocolate, and Honey, Barley with, *94, 97*
  Trail Mix with Toasted Coconut, 210, *211*
Artichokes, detoxifying properties, 39
Arugula
  Beet, and Avocado Salad with Sunflower Seeds, 150, *151*
  and Cherry Salad, Grilled Chicken with, *228,* 229
  and Lentils, Wild Salmon with, 250, *251*
Asparagus
  digestive benefits, 45
  Frittata with Spring Vegetables, 78, *79*
  Steamed Vegetable Salad with Macadamia Dressing, *178,* 179
  Wild Salmon, and Shiitakes in Parchment, 220, *221*
Avocado(s)
  Almonds, and Honey, Black Quinoa with, *94, 96*

Baked Sweet Potato with Greens, 132, *133*
Beet, and Arugula Salad with Sunflower Seeds, 150, *151*
Dark Chocolate "Pudding," *299,* 301
detoxifying properties, 39
Grapefruit, and Salmon Salad, *264,* 265
-Grapefruit Salsa, Seared Halibut Tacos with, 234, *235*
Green Goddess Dip, 200, *201*
Grilled Tofu with Chimichurri on Toast, 218, *219*
healthy fats in, 58
-Orange Salsa, Grilled Salmon and Bok Choy with, 276, *277*
and Pumpkin Seeds, Brussels Sprout Salad with, 154, *155*
Radish, and Basil Soup, 164, *165*
Roasted Golden-Beet, and Watercress Salad, 170, *171*
Roasted Mushroom Tartines with, *168,* 169
Salmon, and Toasted Nori, Brown Rice with, 286, *287*
Steamed Salmon with, 80, *81*
Toasts, Broccoli-Spinach Soup with, *156,* 157
Tofu Scramble with Cotija Cheese and Tortillas, 86, *87*
and Watercress Roll, 202, *203*
-Yogurt Smoothie, 114, *114*
Awareness, focus on, 66

B

Bacteria, beneficial, 45
Banana(s)
  -Apple Buckwheat Muffins, 90, *91*
  Frozen, with Cocoa, *302,* 304
  Mixed Berry "Sorbet," *303,* 305
  Mixed Berry–Tofu Smoothie, 115, *115*

Barley
  about, 50
  with Apricots, Hazelnuts,
    Chocolate, and Honey,
    94, 97
  with Brussels Sprouts, Spinach,
    and Edamame, 142, 143
  cooking methods, 51
  Mixed-Grain and Almond
    Granola, 100, 101
  Shiitake, and Edamame Salad,
    Black Sea Bass with, 240, 241
Basil
  Avocado, and Radish Soup,
    164, 165
  Trout, and Tomatoes in
    Parchment, 270, 271
Bean(s). See also Edamame
  Any-, Dip, Spicy, 186, 188
  Breakfast Vegetable-Miso Soup
    with Chickpeas, 102, 103
  canned, note about, 53
  cooking, 54
  dark, antioxidants in, 41
  glossary of, 55
  health benefits, 53
  rinsing and soaking, 54
  Spicy North African Chicken-
    Chickpea Stew, 272, 273
  suggested uses, 54
  Tofu Scramble with Cotija
    Cheese and Tortillas, 86, 87
  White, Anchovy, Roasted Red-
    Pepper Salad with, 180, 181
  White, and Collard Greens,
    Quesadillas with, 226, 227
  White, and Tuna, 198, 199
  White, Potato, and Kale Stew,
    176, 177
  White, –Roasted Beet
    Hummus, 187, 189
  White, –Spinach Dip, Warm,
    192, 193
Beet(s)
  Apple, and Mint Juice, 111, 111
  Avocado, and Arugula Salad
    with Sunflower Seeds, 150,
    151
  and Buttermilk Soup, 128, 129
  detoxifying properties, 39
  Roasted, –White Bean
    Hummus, 187, 189

Roasted Golden-, Avocado,
    and Watercress Salad, 170,
    171
Berry(ies). See also Blueberry(ies);
    Strawberry(ies)
  -Almond Crisp, 306, 308
  antioxidants in, 41
  Blackberry-Plum Smoothie,
    113, 113
  Mixed, "Sorbet," 303, 305
  Mixed, –Tofu Smoothie, 115,
    115
  Roasted Edamame with
    Cranberries, 192, 193
Blackberry-Plum Smoothie, 113,
    113
Black Cod with Herbs, Zucchini,
    and Whole-Wheat Couscous,
    260, 261
Black Sea Bass with Barley,
    Shiitake, and Edamame Salad,
    240, 241
Blueberry(ies)
  Green Goodness Juice, 112,
    112
  –Green Tea Smoothie, 113, 113
  -Yogurt Smoothie, 114, 114
Bok Choy
  anti-inflammatory properties,
    43
  Buckwheat Noodles, and
    Sweet Potatoes in Miso-
    Lime Broth, 144, 145
  Cauliflower, and Shrimp Stir-
    Fry, Spicy, with Coconut,
    238, 239
  Poached Chicken with, in
    Ginger Broth, 232, 233
  and Salmon, Grilled, with
    Orange-Avocado Salsa, 276,
    277
Brassicas, 39
Breads and toast. See also Tortillas
  Banana-Apple Buckwheat
    Muffins, 90, 91
  Crostini with Fresh Ricotta,
    Cherries, and Lemon Zest,
    84, 85
  Poached Eggs with Roasted
    Tomatoes, 98, 99
  Roasted Mushroom Tartines
    with Avocado, 168, 169

Sardines and Cream Cheese on
    Rye, 92, 93
  Sautéed Mushrooms with
    Toasted Flatbread and Baked
    Eggs, 262, 263
Broccoli
  Breakfast Vegetable-Miso Soup
    with Chickpeas, 102, 103
  and Brown Rice Salad with
    Pumpkin Seeds, 140, 141
  Cauliflower "Rice" Stir-Fry with
    Pumpkin Seeds, 162, 163
  -Spinach Soup with Avocado
    Toasts, 156, 157
Broccoli Rabe, Sautéed Fennel,
    and Ricotta, Brown Rice
    Cakes with, 222, 223
Brown Rice
  about, 50
  and Broccoli Salad with
    Pumpkin Seeds, 140, 141
  Cakes with Sautéed Fennel,
    Broccoli Rabe, and Ricotta,
    222, 223
  cooking methods, 51
  and Edamame, Poached Egg
    with, 230, 231
  with Salmon, Avocado, and
    Toasted Nori, 286, 287
  and Shiitake Mushrooms in
    Parchment, 248, 249
  Spinach, and Tofu Bowl, 236,
    237
Brussels Sprout(s)
  Roasted Vegetables with
    Quinoa, 120, 121
  Salad with Avocado and
    Pumpkin Seeds, 154, 155
  Spinach, and Edamame, Barley
    with, 142, 143
Buckwheat
  about, 50
  cooking methods, 51
  Muffins, Banana-Apple, 90, 91
  Noodles, Bok Choy, and Sweet
    Potatoes in Miso-Lime
    Broth, 144, 145
Bulgur
  about, 50
  cooking methods, 51
  Salad with Pomegranate Seeds,
    166, 167

Buttermilk
and Beet Soup, 128, *129*
-Poached Chicken with
Escarole and Radicchio, *254,
255*

C

Cabbage. *See also* Bok Choy
Watercress and Avocado Roll,
202, *203*
Cancer, 15, 17, 53
Canola oil, cooking with, 58
Carbohydrates, 48
Cardamom Quinoa Porridge
with Pear, 104, *105*
Cardiovascular disease, 15, 53
Carrot(s)
antioxidants in, 41
Beet, Apple, and Mint Juice,
111, *111*
Cleansing Broth, 314
Grapefruit, and Ginger Juice,
111, *111*
and Quinoa, Moroccan-
Steamed Salmon with, 290,
291
Spinach, and Green Bean Soup
with Dill, *182*, 183
Steamed Vegetable Salad with
Macadamia Dressing, *178*,
179
and Sweet Peppers, Roasted,
with Orange and Hazelnuts,
148, *149*
Watercress and Avocado Roll,
202, *203*
Cauliflower
Bok Choy, and Shrimp Stir-Fry,
Spicy, with Coconut, 238,
239
"Rice" Stir-Fry with Pumpkin
Seeds, *162*, 163
Roasted, Simple, 204, *205*
Roasted, Yogurt Dip, *186*, 188
Soup, Pureed, 152, *153*
Cayenne pepper, 39
Celery
Caramelized Fennel, and
Sardine Pasta, 246, *247*
Cleansing Broth, 314
detoxifying properties, 39

Fennel, Sunchoke, and Green
Apple Salad, 122, *123*
Chai Tea Latte, *311*, 313
Cheese
Brown Rice Cakes with
Sautéed Fennel, Broccoli
Rabe, and Ricotta, *222*,
223
Cotija, and Tortillas, Tofu
Scramble with, 86, *87*
Cream, and Sardines on Rye,
92, *93*
cream, healthy swap for, 47
Crostini with Fresh Ricotta,
Cherries, and Lemon Zest,
84, *85*
Goat, Farro, and Pea Shoot
Salad, *126*, 127
Melon with Feta and Black
Pepper, 208, *209*
Quesadillas with Collard
Greens and White Beans,
226, *227*
Spinach Tart with Olive-Oil
Cracker Crust, 278, *279*
Squash Salad with Tomatoes,
Zucchini Blossoms, and
Ricotta, 138, *139*
Yogurt, Garlic-Herb, 194, *195*
Cherry(ies)
and Arugula Salad, Grilled
Chicken with, *228*, 229
-Coconut Smoothie, 112, *112*
Fresh Ricotta, and Lemon Zest,
Crostini with, 84, *85*
sweet, antioxidants in, 41
Chicken
Breast, Almond-Crusted, with
Spinach, 258, *259*
Breasts, Ginger-Scallion, in
Parchment, 284, *285*
Buttermilk-Poached, with
Escarole and Radicchio, *254,
255*
-Chickpea Stew, Spicy North
African, *272*, 273
Grilled, with Cherry and
Arugula Salad, *228*, 229
Grilled, with Cucumber,
Radish, and Cherry Tomato
Relish, *244*, 245

Paillards with Squash and
Spinach, *216*, 217
Poached, with Bok Choy in
Ginger Broth, 232, *233*
Soup, Almond, with Sweet
Potato, Collards, and Ginger,
288, *289*
Stew, Mediterranean, with
Couscous, 252, *253*
Stock, 314
and Tomato Soup, Spicy
Indian, 224, *225*
Chiles, roasting, 314
Chocolate
Apricots, Hazelnuts, and
Honey, Barley with, *94*, 97
-Coconut Macaroons, *298*, 300
dark, antioxidants in, 41, 47
Dark, Bark with Hazelnuts,
298, 300
Dark, "Pudding," *299*, 301
Dark, Spiced Hot, *310*, 312
Dark, Truffles, *299*, 301
Frozen Bananas with Cocoa,
302, 304
milk, healthy swap for, 47
-Walnut Brownies, *307*, 309
Cholesterol, 17, 49, 53, 56,
57, 58
Cilantro
Black Cod with Herbs,
Zucchini, and Whole-Wheat
Couscous, 260, *261*
Creamy Summer Squash Soup
with, *172*, 173
detoxifying properties, 39
Moroccan-Steamed Salmon
with Quinoa and Carrots,
290, *291*
Citrus. *See also specific citrus
fruits*
detoxifying properties, 39
flavoring dishes with, 59
Salad with Pomegranate, *294*,
296
segmenting, 314
Cloves, 41
Cocoa powder, 41
Coconut
Breakfast Pudding with
Sautéed Nectarines, 76, *77*

-Cherry Smoothie, 112, *112*
-Chocolate Macaroons, *298,* 300
digestive benefits, 45
oil, cooking with, 58
oil, digestive benefits, 45
Pineapple, and Flaxseed, Millet with, *94, 95*
Pistachio-Stuffed Dates with, *294, 296*
Spicy Cauliflower, Bok Choy, and Shrimp Stir-Fry with, 238, *239*
Toasted, Trail Mix with, 210, *211*
toasting, 314
water, hydrating properties, 29
-Water Ice Pops, *303,* 305
Water–Mango Smoothie, 116, *116*
Cod, Shrimp, and Fennel Soup with Tomatoes, 274, *275*
Coffee
    antioxidants in, 41
    omitting, during cleanse, 61
Collard Greens
    and Lemon, Spaghetti with, *268,* 269
    Sweet Potato, and Ginger, Almond Chicken Soup with, 288, *289*
    and White Beans, Quesadillas with, 226, *227*
Couscous
    Mediterranean Chicken Stew with, 252, *253*
    Whole-Wheat, Herbs, and Zucchini, Black Cod with, 260, *261*
Cranberries, Roasted Edamame with, 192, *193*
Croutons, healthy swap for, 47
Cucumber(s)
    Apple, and Lemon Juice, 110, *110*
    Grilled Tofu with Chimichurri on Toast, 218, *219*
    -Pear Juice, 116, *116*
    Radish, and Cherry Tomato Relish, Grilled Chicken with, *244, 245*
    Spinach-Apple Juice, 113, *113*

and Yogurt Dip, Spicy, 200, *201*
and Yogurt Soup, 128, *129*

D
Dairy. *See also specific dairy products*
    fermented, digestive benefits, 45
    full-fat, note about, 56
    omitting, during cleanse, 61
Date(s)
    -Almond Smoothie, 114, *114*
    No-Bake Oat Bars with Strawberries, *295, 297*
    Pistachio-Stuffed, with Coconut, *294, 296*
Dehydration, 29
Detoxifying drinks, 110–11
Detoxifying foods, 39
Detox plans
    how they work, 61
    "six to skip" foods, 61
    3-Day Action Plan, 62–63
    21-Day Action Plan, 64–69
Diabetes, 15, 49, 53
Digestive aid foods, 45

E
Edamame
    about, 55
    Barley, and Shiitake Salad, Black Sea Bass with, *240,* 241
    Brussels Sprouts, and Spinach, Barley with, *142,* 143
    and Rice, Poached Egg with, 230, *231*
    Roasted, with Cranberries, 192, *193*
Egg(s)
    Baked, and Toasted Flatbread, Sautéed Mushrooms with, 262, *263*
    Dashi-Poached Sweet Potatoes and Greens, *136, 137*
    Frittata with Spring Vegetables, 78, *79*
    Hard-Cooked, with Mustard, 190, *191*
    Mushroom and Microgreen Omelet, *106, 107*

Poached, Swiss Chard Salad with, *130,* 131
Poached, with Rice and Edamame, 230, *231*
Poached, with Roasted Tomatoes, 98, *99*
Energizing smoothies, 114–15
Escarole
    Mediterranean Chicken Stew with Couscous, 252, *253*
    and Radicchio, Buttermilk-Poached Chicken with, *254,* 255
Exercise, 21, 64, 66, 68

F
Farro
    about, 50
    cooking methods, 51
    Pea Shoot, and Goat Cheese Salad, *126,* 127
    and Roasted Sweet Potato Salad, 174, *175*
    Spaghetti with Fresh Tomatoes and Marcona Almonds, *256,* 257
Fats, dietary
    "good" versus "bad," 56
    healthy types of, 57–58
    saturated, 17, 57
    trans fats, 57
Fennel
    Caramelized, Celery, and Sardine Pasta, 246, *247*
    detoxifying properties, 39
    and Grapefruit, Poached Salmon with, *282, 283*
    Sautéed, Broccoli Rabe, and Ricotta, Brown Rice Cakes with, *222, 223*
    Shrimp, and Cod Soup with Tomatoes, 274, *275*
    Steamed Vegetable Salad with Macadamia Dressing, *178,* 179
    Sunchoke, and Green Apple Salad, 122, *123*
    Ultra-Green Juice, 110, *110*
Fermented foods, 45

Fiber
  in digestive-aid foods, 45
  flushing out toxins with, 39
  in legumes, 53
  recommended daily
    amounts, 23
  types of, 23
  in whole grains, 48
Fig(s)
  Honey-Caramelized, with
    Yogurt, 82, 83
  and Walnut Biscotti, 306, 308
Fish. See also Anchovy(ies);
    Salmon; Sardine(s)
  Black Cod with Herbs,
    Zucchini, and Whole-Wheat
    Couscous, 260, 261
  Black Sea Bass with Barley,
    Shiitake, and Edamame
    Salad, 240, 241
  cold-water, anti-inflammatory
    properties, 43
  oily, healthy fats in, 58
  Seared Halibut Tacos with
    Grapefruit-Avocado Salsa,
    234, 235
  Shrimp, Cod, and Fennel Soup
    with Tomatoes, 274, 275
  Stock, 315
  Trout, Tomatoes, and Basil in
    Parchment, 270, 271
  Tuna and White Beans, 198,
    199
Fish sauce, about, 59
Flavor-enhancing foods, 59
Flaxseed
  detoxifying properties, 39
  digestive benefits, 45
  Pineapple, and Coconut, Millet
    with, 94, 95
Fluid intake, 29
Food allergies, 27, 37
Food intolerances, 27, 37
Food journals, 27
Food labels, 33
Food shopping, 31, 33
Free radicals, 41
Fruit. See also Berry(ies); Citrus;
    specific fruits
  and Almond Alpine Muesli,
    88, 89
  Dried, and Nut Bites, 210, 211

frozen, buying, 15
new, experimenting with, 17

G
Garlic
  Cleansing Broth, 314
  -Herb Yogurt Cheese, 194, 195
Ginger
  Aloe-Vera, and Orange
    Smoothie, 117, 117
  Broth, Poached Chicken with
    Bok Choy in, 232, 233
  digestive benefits, 45
  Grapefruit, and Carrot Juice,
    111, 111
  Pear, and Oat Smoothie, 115,
    115
  -Scallion Chicken Breasts in
    Parchment, 284, 285
  Spicy Indian Chicken and
    Tomato Soup, 224, 225
  Strawberry, and Grapefruit
    Smoothie, 110, 110
  Sweet Potato, and Collards,
    Almond Chicken Soup with,
    288, 289
  -Watermelon Juice, 117, 117
Gluten-free pastas, 52
Gluten sensitivities, 61
Golden Rules
  boost energy with lean
    protein, 25
  choosing whole foods over
    processed, 15
  embracing a plant-based
    diet, 17
  engaging in an active
    lifestyle, 21
  establish smart meal-planning
    habits, 31
  getting enough fiber, 23
  know what you are buying, 33
  maintain healthy perspective,
    35
  pay attention to how you
    feel, 27
  practice mindful eating, 19
  stay hydrated, 29
Grains. See also Barley; Brown
    Rice; Farro; Oat(s); Quinoa
  Banana-Apple Buckwheat
    Muffins, 90, 91

Bulgur Salad with
    Pomegranate Seeds, 166, 167
  buying whole-grain products,
    23, 49
  cooking methods, 51
  digestive benefits, 45
  glossary of, 50
  Grapes, and Sage, Roasted
    Squash with, 146, 147
  health benefits, 49
  Millet with Pineapple,
    Coconut, and Flaxseed,
    94, 95
  Mixed-, and Almond Granola,
    100, 101
  whole versus refined, 48
Granita, Watermelon-Lime, 302,
    304
Granola
  Mixed-Grain and Almond,
    100, 101
  and Yogurt, Roasted Plums
    with, 295, 297
Grapefruit
  -Avocado Salsa, Seared Halibut
    Tacos with, 234, 235
  Carrot, and Ginger Juice, 111,
    111
  and Fennel, Poached Salmon
    with, 282, 283
  Salmon, and Avocado Salad,
    264, 265
  Strawberry, and Ginger
    Smoothie, 110, 110
Grapes
  antioxidants in, 41
  Grains, and Sage, Roasted
    Squash with, 146, 147
  and Kiwi, Frozen, 202, 203
Green Bean(s)
  Carrot, and Spinach Soup with
    Dill, 182, 183
  Steamed, with Lemon, 198,
    199
  Steamed Vegetable Salad with
    Macadamia Dressing, 178,
    179
Greens. See also Arugula; Collard
    Greens; Kale; Spinach;
    Watercress
  Baked Sweet Potato with, 132,
    133

Buttermilk-Poached Chicken with Escarole and Radicchio, *254, 255*
dandelion, detoxifying properties, 39
dark leafy, antioxidants in, 41
Dashi-Poached Sweet Potatoes and, *136, 137*
Green Machine Smoothie, 111, *111*
iceberg compared with Romaine, 47
Mediterranean Chicken Stew with Couscous, 252, *253*
Mushroom and Microgreen Omelet, *106,* 107
Pineapple-Spinach Juice, 117, *117*
and Radishes, Roasted, 204, *205*
Swiss Chard Salad with Poached Egg, *130,* 131

H
Halibut, Seared, Tacos with Grapefruit-Avocado Salsa, 234, *235*
Harissa
    Bell Pepper, and Yogurt Soup, 164, *165*
    recipe for, 315
Hazelnuts
    Apricots, Chocolate, and Honey, Barley with, *94, 97*
    Dark Chocolate Bark with, *298,* 300
    and Orange, Roasted Sweet Peppers and Carrots with, 148, *149*
    toasting, 314
Health claims, note about, 15
Healthy habits, forming, 35, 68
Heart disease, 15, 17, 49, 56, 57, 58
Herb(s). *See also specific herbs*
    anti-inflammatory properties, 43
    fresh, flavoring dishes with, 59
    -Garlic Yogurt Cheese, 194, *195*
    Green Goddess Dip, 200, *201*

Honey
    -Caramelized Figs with Yogurt, 82, 83
    digestive benefits, 45
Hummus, Roasted Beet–White Bean, *187,* 189
Hydrating drinks, 116–17
Hydration, 29

I
Inflammation-fighting foods, 43

J
Junk food, 15

K
Kale
    Chips with Sesame Seeds, 194, *195*
    Green Goodness Juice, 112, *112*
    Green Machine Smoothie, 111, *111*
    Poached Egg with Rice and Edamame, 230, *231*
    and Red Onion, Roasted Portobellos with, *158, 159*
    -Sunflower Smoothie, Sweet, 115, *115*
    Ultra-Green Juice, 110, *110*
    White Bean, and Potato Stew, 176, *177*
Kamut
    about, 50
    cooking methods, 51
Kefir, benefits of, 45
Kiwi
    antioxidants in, 41
    and Grapes, Frozen, 202, *203*

L
Legumes. *See also* Bean(s); Lentil(s)
    cooking, 54
    digestive benefits, 45
    general health benefits, 53
    glossary of, 55
    rinsing and soaking, 54
    suggested uses, 54
Lentil(s)
    about, 55
    and Arugula, Wild Salmon with, 250, *251*

Burgers with Lettuce and Yogurt, *242,* 243
    Red, Soup with Turnip and Parsley, 266, *267*
Lettuce
    Green Machine Smoothie, 111, *111*
    iceberg compared with Romaine, 47
    Pineapple-Spinach Juice, 117, *117*
Liver-cleansing foods, 39
Lymphatic system, 21

M
Macadamia(s)
    Dressing, Steamed Vegetable Salad with, *178,* 179
    No-Bake Oat Bars with Strawberries, *295,* 297
Macaroons, Coconut-Chocolate, *298,* 300
Mango
    Aloe-Vera, Ginger, and Orange Smoothie, 117, *117*
    Coconut-Water Ice Pops, *303,* 305
    –Coconut Water Smoothie, 116, *116*
    Green Machine Smoothie, 111, *111*
Mayonnaise, healthy swap for, 47
Meal planning, 31
Meals, planning, 31
Meat, note about, 25
Melon
    with Feta and Black Pepper, 208, *209*
    -Mint Smoothie, 116, *116*
    Ultra-Green Juice, 110, *110*
    Watermelon-Ginger Juice, 117, *117*
    Watermelon-Lime Granita, *302,* 304
Milk, Almond, 315
Millet
    about, 50
    cooking methods, 51
    with Pineapple, Coconut, and Flaxseed, *94, 95*
Mindful eating, 19

Mint
  Beet, and Apple Juice, 111, *111*
  Black Cod with Herbs,
    Zucchini, and Whole-Wheat
    Couscous, 260, *261*
  Bulgur Salad with
    Pomegranate Seeds, 166, *167*
  digestive benefits, 45
  and Lemon, Pureed Pea Dip
    with, 208, *209*
  -Melon Smoothie, 116, *116*
  Zucchini, and Pistachios,
    Quinoa Salad with, 134,
    135
Miso
  digestive benefits, 45
  flavoring dishes with, 59
  -Lime Broth, Buckwheat
    Noodles, Bok Choy, and
    Sweet Potatoes in, 144, *145*
  -Vegetable Soup with
    Chickpeas, Breakfast, 102,
    103
Monounsaturated fats, 57
Mushroom(s)
  Black Sea Bass with Barley,
    Shiitake, and Edamame
    Salad, *240*, 241
  button, healthy swap for, 47
  Ginger-Scallion Chicken
    Breasts in Parchment, 284,
    285
  and Microgreen Omelet, *106*,
    107
  Roasted, Tartines with
    Avocado, *168*, 169
  Roasted Portobellos with Kale
    and Red Onion, *158*, 159
  Sautéed, with Toasted
    Flatbread and Baked Eggs,
    262, *263*
  Shiitake, and Brown Rice in
    Parchment, *248*, 249
  shiitake, anti-inflammatory
    properties, 43, 47
  Wild Salmon, Asparagus, and
    Shiitakes in Parchment, 220,
    221

N
Nectarines, Sautéed, Coconut
  Breakfast Pudding with, 76, 77

Noodles
  Buckwheat, Bok Choy, and
    Sweet Potatoes in Miso-
    Lime Broth, 144, *145*
  Soba with Salmon and
    Watercress, 214, *215*
Nori, Toasted, Salmon, and
  Avocado, Brown Rice with,
  286, *287*
Nori sprinkles, about, 59
Nutrient-rich foods
  antioxidant powerhouses, 41
  digestive aids, 45
  inflammation fighters, 43
  super detoxifiers, 39
Nut(s). *See also* Almond(s);
  Hazelnuts; Pistachio(s);
  Walnut(s)
  and Dried Fruit Bites, 210,
    211
  healthy fats in, 58
  No-Bake Oat Bars with
    Strawberries, *295*, 297
  pecans, antioxidants in, 41
  Steamed Vegetable Salad with
    Macadamia Dressing, *178*,
    179
  toasting, 314
  Trail Mix with Toasted
    Coconut, 210, *211*

O
Oat(s)
  about, 50
  Bars, No-Bake, with
    Strawberries, *295*, 297
  Berry-Almond Crisp, *306*,
    308
  Coconut Breakfast Pudding
    with Sautéed Nectarines,
    76, 77
  cooking methods, 51
  Fruit and Almond Alpine
    Muesli, *88*, 89
  Mixed-Grain and Almond
    Granola, *100*, 101
  Oatmeal-Raisin Cookies, *307*,
    309
  and Peanut Butter, Apple with,
    206, *207*
  Pear, and Ginger Smoothie,
    115, *115*

Oils
  coconut, 45, 58
  for cooking, 58
  nut and seed, drizzling over
    dishes, 59
  olive, 41, 58
  safflower, 57, 58
Olive oil
  antioxidants in, 41
  cooking with, 58
Omega-3 fatty acids, 57, 58
Omega-3 supplements, 57
Omega-3 vinaigrette,
  preparing, 59
Omelet, Mushroom and
  Microgreen, *106*, 107
Orange(s)
  Aloe-Vera, and Ginger
    Smoothie, 117, *117*
  -Avocado Salsa, Grilled Salmon
    and Bok Choy with, 276, *277*
  Fruit and Almond Alpine
    Muesli, *88*, 89
  and Hazelnuts, Roasted Sweet
    Peppers and Carrots with,
    148, *149*
  Watercress, and Sardine Salad,
    280, *281*
Organic food labels, 33

P
Pantry foods
  flavor enhancers, 59
  healthy fats, 56–58
  legumes, 53–55
  smart ingredient swaps, 47
  whole grains, 48–52
Papaya
  anti-inflammatory
    properties, 43
  Coconut-Water Ice Pops, *303*,
    305
  Smoothie, Spiced, 112, *112*
Parsley
  Cleansing Broth, 314
  Grilled Tofu with Chimichurri
    on Toast, 218, *219*
  and Turnip, Red Lentil Soup
    with, 266, *267*
Pasta
  Caramelized Fennel, Celery,
    and Sardine, 246, *247*

cooking, 52
Farro Spaghetti with Fresh
   Tomatoes and Marcona
   Almonds, *256*, *257*
fiber in, 52
gluten-free varieties, 52
serving sizes, 52
Spaghetti with Collard Greens
   and Lemon, *268*, *269*
whole-grain varieties, 52
Peach, White, and Heirloom
   Tomato Salad, 160, *161*
Pea Dip, Puree, with Mint and
   Lemon, 208, *209*
Peanut Butter and Oats, Apple
   with, 206, *207*
Pear
   Cardamom Quinoa Porridge
      with, 104, *105*
   -Cucumber Juice, 116, *116*
   Oat, and Ginger Smoothie,
      115, *115*
Pea Shoot, Farro, and Goat
   Cheese Salad, *126*, 127
Pecans, antioxidants in, 41
Pepper(s)
   Bell, Yogurt, and Harissa Soup,
      164, *165*
   Cauliflower "Rice" Stir-Fry with
      Pumpkin Seeds, *162*, 163
   dried, flavoring dishes with, 59
   Red, and Walnut Dip with
      Pomegranate, *187*, 189
   Roasted Red-, Salad with
      Anchovy White Beans, 180,
      181
   roasting, 314
   Sweet, and Carrots, Roasted,
      with Orange and Hazelnuts,
      148, *149*
Pineapple
   Coconut, and Flaxseed, Millet
      with, *94*, 95
   Coconut-Water Ice Pops, *303*,
      305
   Green Machine Smoothie, 111,
      111
   -Spinach Juice, 117, *117*
Pistachio(s)
   healthy fats in, 58
   Honey-Caramelized Figs with
      Yogurt, *82*, 83

-Stuffed Dates with Coconut,
   294, 296
Trail Mix with Toasted
   Coconut, 210, *211*
Zucchini, and Mint, Quinoa
   Salad with, 134, *135*
Plant-based diets, 17
Plum(s)
   antioxidants in, 41
   -Blackberry Smoothie, 113, *113*
   Roasted, with Yogurt and
      Granola, *295*, 297
Polyunsaturated fats, 57
Pomegranate
   Citrus Salad with, *294*, 296
   Red Pepper and Walnut Dip
      with, *187*, 189
   Seeds, Bulgur Salad with, 166,
      167
Portion sizes, 19
Potato. *See also* Sweet Potato(es)
   compared with sweet
      potatoes, 47
   and Watercress Soup, 124, *125*
   White Bean, and Kale Stew,
      176, *177*
Processed foods, 15, 61
Protein
   boosting energy with, 25
   in legumes, 53
Pudding, Coconut Breakfast,
   with Sautéed Nectarines,
   76, 77
"Pudding," Dark Chocolate, *299*,
   301
Pumpkin Seeds
   and Avocado, Brussels Sprout
      Salad with, 154, *155*
   Broccoli and Brown Rice Salad
      with, 140, *141*
   Cauliflower "Rice" Stir-Fry
      with, *162*, 163
   Spiced, 196, *197*
   toasting, 314

Q

Quesadillas with Collard Greens
   and White Beans, 226, 227
Quinoa
   about, 50
   Black, with Avocado, Almonds,
      and Honey, *94*, 96

Cardamom Porridge with Pear,
   104, *105*
and Carrots, Moroccan-
   Steamed Salmon with, 290,
   291
cooking methods, 51
Roasted Vegetables with, 120,
   121
Salad with Zucchini, Mint, and
   Pistachios, 134, *135*

R

Radicchio and Escarole,
   Buttermilk-Poached Chicken
   with, *254*, 255
Radish(es)
   Avocado, and Basil Soup, 164,
      165
   Cucumber, and Cherry
      Tomato Relish, Grilled
      Chicken with, *244*, 245
   and Greens, Roasted, 204, *205*
Raisin(s)
   Bulgur Salad with
      Pomegranate Seeds, 166,
      167
   -Oatmeal Cookies, *307*, 309
Rice. *See* Brown Rice

S

Safflower oil, cooking with,
   57, 58
Salmon
   Avocado, and Toasted Nori,
      Brown Rice with, 286, *287*
   Grapefruit, and Avocado Salad,
      264, 265
   Grilled, and Bok Choy with
      Orange-Avocado Salsa, 276,
      277
   Moroccan-Steamed, with
      Quinoa and Carrots, 290,
      291
   Poached, with Fennel and
      Grapefruit, *282*, 283
   Steamed, with Avocado, 80, *81*
   and Watercress, Soba with, 214,
      215
   Wild, Asparagus, and Shiitakes
      in Parchment, 220, *221*
   Wild, with Lentils and
      Arugula, 250, *251*

Salt, seasoning with, 59
Sardine(s)
    Caramelized Fennel, and
        Celery Pasta, 246, 247
    and Cream Cheese on Rye,
        92, 93
    Salad with Lemon and Herbs,
        190, 191
    Watercress, and Orange Salad,
        280, 281
Saturated fats, 17, 57
Seeds. See also specific seeds
    Dried Fruit and Nut Bites, 210,
        211
    flavoring dishes with, 59
    toasting, 314
Sesame Seeds
    Dried Fruit and Nut Bites, 210,
        211
    Kale Chips with, 194, 195
    toasting, 314
Shellfish. See Shrimp
Shopping strategies, 31, 33
Shrimp
    Cauliflower, and Bok Choy
        Stir-Fry, Spicy, with Coconut,
        238, 239
    Cod, and Fennel Soup with
        Tomatoes, 274, 275
Sleep, 21, 62
"Sorbet," Mixed Berry, 303, 305
Sour cream, healthy swap for, 47
Spelt
    about, 50
    cooking methods, 51
Spices, anti-inflammatory
    properties, 43
Spinach
    Almond-Crusted Chicken
        Breast with, 258, 259
    -Apple Juice, 113, 113
    -Broccoli Soup with Avocado
        Toasts, 156, 157
    Brussels Sprouts, and
        Edamame, Barley with, 142,
        143
    Carrot, and Green Bean Soup
        with Dill, 182, 183
    Cleansing Broth, 314
    Green Goodness Juice, 112,
        112
    -Pineapple Juice, 117, 117

and Squash, Chicken Paillards
    with, 216, 217
Tart with Olive-Oil Cracker
    Crust, 278, 279
Tofu, and Brown Rice Bowl,
    236, 237
–White Bean Dip, Warm, 192,
    193
Split peas, about, 55
Squash. See also Zucchini
    Roasted, with Grains, Grapes,
        and Sage, 146, 147
    Roasted Vegetables with
        Quinoa, 120, 121
    Salad with Tomatoes, Zucchini
        Blossoms, and Ricotta, 138,
        139
    and Spinach, Chicken Paillards
        with, 216, 217
    Summer, Soup, Creamy, with
        Cilantro, 172, 173
    winter, antioxidants in, 41
Stocks
    Chicken, 314
    Cleansing Broth, 314
    Fish, 315
    Vegetable, 314–15
Strawberry(ies)
    Grapefruit, and Ginger
        Smoothie, 110, 110
    No-Bake Oat Bars with, 295,
        297
    Sliced, and Yogurt, Whole-
        Wheat Waffles with, 74, 75
Stress, 21
Sugar, omitting, during
    cleanse, 61
"Sugar-free" claims, 33
Sunchoke, Fennel, and Green
    Apple Salad, 122, 123
Sunflower
    -Kale Smoothie, Sweet, 115,
        115
    Seeds, Beet, Avocado, and
        Arugula Salad with, 150, 151
    seeds, toasting, 314
Sweet Potato(es)
    antioxidants in, 41
    Baked, with Greens, 132, 133
    Buckwheat Noodles, and Bok
        Choy in Miso-Lime Broth,
        144, 145

Chips, 206, 207
Cleansing Broth, 314
Collards, and Ginger, Almond
    Chicken Soup with, 288,
    289
compared with potatoes, 47
Dashi-Poached, and Greens,
    136, 137
Roasted, and Farro Salad, 174,
    175
Swiss Chard
    Baked Sweet Potato with
        Greens, 132, 133
    Salad with Poached Egg, 130,
        131

T

Tacos, Seared Halibut, with
    Grapefruit-Avocado Salsa, 234,
    235
Tart, Spinach, with Olive-Oil
    Cracker Crust, 278, 279
Tea
    antioxidants in, 41
    Chai, Latte, 311, 313
    Green, –Blueberry Smoothie,
        113, 113
Tofu
    Dashi-Poached Sweet Potatoes
        and Greens, 136, 137
    Grilled, with Chimichurri on
        Toast, 218, 219
    –Mixed Berry Smoothie, 115,
        115
    pressing, 314
    Scramble with Cotija Cheese
        and Tortillas, 86, 87
    Spinach, and Brown Rice
        Bowl, 236, 237
Tomato(es)
    Cherry, Cucumber, and Radish
        Relish, Grilled Chicken
        with, 244, 245
    and Chicken Soup, Spicy
        Indian, 224, 225
    Fresh, and Marcona Almonds,
        Farro Spaghetti with, 256,
        257
    Heirloom, and White Peach
        Salad, 160, 161
    paste, flavoring dishes
        with, 59

Roasted, Poached Eggs with, 98, *99*

Shrimp, Cod, and Fennel Soup with, 274, *275*

Trout, and Basil in Parchment, 270, *271*

Zucchini Blossoms, and Ricotta, Squash Salad with, 138, *139*

Tortillas

and Cotija Cheese, Tofu Scramble with, 86, *87*

Quesadillas with Collard Greens and White Beans, 226, *227*

Seared Halibut Tacos with Grapefruit-Avocado Salsa, 234, *235*

Trail Mix with Toasted Coconut, 210, *211*

Trans fats, 57

Trout, Tomatoes, and Basil in Parchment, 270, *271*

Truffles, Dark Chocolate, *299,* 301

Tuna and White Beans, 198, *199*

Turmeric, digestive benefits, 45

Turnip and Parsley, Red Lentil Soup with, 266, *267*

V

Vegetable(s). *See also specific vegetables*

fermented, digestive benefits, 45

frozen, buying, 15

-Miso Soup with Chickpeas, Breakfast, 102, *103*

new, experimenting with, 17

sea, detoxifying properties, 39

seasonal, buying, 31

Spring, Frittata with, 78, *79*

Steamed, Salad with Macadamia Dressing, *178,* 179

Stock, 314–15

Vinaigrette, omega-3, preparing, 59

Vinegar, flavoring dishes with, 59

W

Waffles, Whole-Wheat, with Sliced Strawberries and Yogurt, 74, *75*

Walnut(s)

adding to salads, 47

anti-inflammatory properties, 43

Banana-Apple Buckwheat Muffins, 90, *91*

Chocolate Brownies, *307,* 309

and Fig Biscotti, *306,* 308

healthy fats in, 58

and Red Pepper Dip with Pomegranate, *187,* 189

Water, importance of, 29

Watercress

and Avocado Roll, 202, *203*

detoxifying properties, 39

and Potato Soup, 124, *125*

Roasted Golden-Beet, and Avocado Salad, 170, *171*

and Salmon, Soba with, 214, *215*

Sardine, and Orange Salad, 280, *281*

Watermelon

-Ginger Juice, 117, *117*

-Lime Granita, *302,* 304

Wheat berries

about, 50

cooking methods, 51

Y

Yogurt

Almond-Date Smoothie, 114, *114*

-Avocado Smoothie, 114, *114*

Bell Pepper, and Harissa Soup, 164, *165*

-Blueberry Smoothie, 114, *114*

Cheese, Garlic-Herb, 194, *195*

and Cucumber Dip, Spicy, 200, *201*

and Cucumber Soup, 128, *129*

digestive benefits, 45

Fruit and Almond Alpine Muesli, *88,* 89

and Granola, Roasted Plums with, *295,* 297

Honey-Caramelized Figs with, *82,* 83

and Lettuce, Lentil Burgers with, *242,* 243

Roasted Cauliflower Dip, *186,* 188

and Sliced Strawberries, Whole-Wheat Waffles with, 74, *75*

Z

Zucchini

Blossoms, Squash, and Ricotta, Squash Salad with, 138, *139*

Frittata with Spring Vegetables, 78, *79*

Herbs, and Whole-Wheat Couscous, Black Cod with, 260, *261*

Mint, and Pistachios, Quinoa Salad with, 134, *135*